# AMERICAN PUNCTUATION

By

GEORGE SUMMEY, Jr.

THE AGRICULTURAL AND MECHANICAL COLLEGE OF TEXAS

THE RONALD PRESS COMPANY ⸱ NEW YORK

Copyright, 1949, by
THE RONALD PRESS COMPANY

2

Library of Congress Catalog Card Number: 49-7374
PRINTED IN THE UNITED STATES OF AMERICA

*To*

THE LYNX-EYED AMERICAN FRATERNITY
OF COPY EDITORS AND PROOFREADERS

# PREFACE

*American Punctuation* is a study of punctuation in its relationship to the art of writing. Its conclusions are based upon actual practice observed in good current American prose, exclusive of fiction and advertising. Where there are generalizations, they are based upon a variety of material selected from editorials, news stories, and articles appearing in the better newspapers and magazines. Such a study, however, tends to keep generalizations to a minimum, for the investigator must recognize that in many cases practice may vary without being wrong.

I have purposely said little about the punctuation of fiction, radio script, or advertising, because some practices acceptable in these fields differ from the customs of style observed by the writers of nonfiction. Also omitted, as beyond the province of my subject, is the consideration of style in capitalization, italic, boldface, or small capitals—these matters being best handled by professional printers, as in John Benbow's *Manuscript & Proof* and in the manuals published by the University of Chicago Press and the United States Government Printing Office.

*American Punctuation* should have practical worth for all who are seriously interested in writing: for student and teacher, for reporter and rewrite man, for staff writer and free lance, for proofreader, copy reader, and editor. It should be a useful reference on the English and journalism shelves of school and college libraries and in the libraries of newspapers, magazines, and publishing houses.

The greater part of the book (Chapters 1–8) deals with structural punctuation—the use of paragraph breaks and

the various marks used between or within sentences to make
the writer's meaning clear at sight. Chapters 9–11 deal
briefly with quotation marks, hyphens, apostrophes, and abbreviation periods. The Appendix, "A Cross Section of Patterns and Punctuation," upon which many of the conclusions in the text are based, gives some information about
frequencies of marks per sentence, relative frequencies of the
various marks, structural types of sentences, kinds of sentence beginnings, and the ways in which certain groups are
handled.

Though *American Punctuation* uses some of the material
of my earlier book, *Modern Punctuation* (Oxford University
Press, New York, 1919), it is not a revision or abridgment
but a new book. I have checked by recent observation every
statement in the old book, and have corrected some errors
that were pointed out by reviewers and certain statements
that were true in 1918 but are no longer true today.

For useful material and constructive criticism, I am
especially indebted to the late Dr. James W. Bright of Johns
Hopkins University, to Dr. Robert L. Ramsay of the University of Missouri, and to Miss Elizabeth P. Cleveland of
Madison College at Harrisonburg, Virginia. For their suggestions and assistance during the writing of the manuscript,
I am under obligation to my colleagues Dr. John Paul Abbott
and Dr. Stewart S. Morgan. I acknowledge also my obligation for permission to quote from numerous sources, both
books and periodicals. Specific acknowledgment of such copyright material is made where each extract appears.

GEORGE SUMMEY, JR.

College Station, Texas
September 1948

# CONTENTS

# AMERICAN PUNCTUATION

# CHAPTER 1

# GENERAL CONSIDERATIONS

Punctuation is the use of certain conventional marks for the purpose of making written matter clear at sight. The term includes (1) structural punctuation—the use of marks to indicate paragraph and sentence relations, and grouping within sentences, (2) the use of quotation marks and marks of editorial interpolation and ellipsis, and (3) the use of certain orthographical or word points—division hyphen, compounding hyphen, apostrophe, and abbreviation period. The principal subject of the book is structural punctuation.[1]

## Good Structural Punctuation

Skilful punctuation—including the omission of useless and obstructive punctuation—makes clear at a glance the relations and sometimes the junctions of word groups, and often indicates their relative weights. A badly chosen mark annoys the reader by asking him to do the writer's work of grouping the material, or distorts the intended emphasis. Omission of a needed mark puzzles the reader momentarily and gives him the trouble of guessing at the writer's intention. Useless marks check the progress of reading and suggest groupings and relations that are not intended.

---

[1] The structural marks included are period, question mark, exclamation mark, comma, dash, semicolon, colon, parentheses, brackets, and suspension dots. Asterisks are only briefly mentioned. Not included are marks of pronunciation (dieresis, cedilla, etc.), ditto marks, the caret, the brace, the asterism, or reference indexes such as the star-and-dagger series and superior letters or figures.

3

## Using the Right Mark

The notion that there is only one correct way of punctuating a given word pattern is true only in limited degree. Skilful writers have learned that they must make alert and successful choices between periods and semicolons, semicolons and commas, commas and dashes, dashes and parentheses, according to meaning and intended emphasis. To do this well, they must know what a mark can do and can't do, and what signals of meaning, emphasis, and relations the various marks will clearly give. For example, the dash is more strongly suspensive than the comma; the colon is anticipatory ("See what's coming"), and the semicolon is not, though the wording with it may be. Members of a compound sentence with *and* are fused together if there is no mark before the connective, and are made more distinct by a comma and still more distinct by a semicolon. The options for various patterns within the acceptable area of choice are outlined in the following chapters.

## Supplying All Needed Marks

Though it is important to write so well that a low average number of marks per sentence will serve the purpose, economy by omission of a needed mark is false economy. For example:

If, instead of the estate passing to the widow as a lump sum, a trust is created the above-mentioned expenses are not eliminated. The net estate would pass into the hands of the selected trustee and his commissions, additional court costs and administration expenses would mean further deductions. [In the first sentence, a comma after *created* would help the reader to get the meaning. In the second sentence, a comma is needed after *selected trustee* to mark the junction between sentence members, and another comma would be useful after *court costs.*]

Dr. Albert Einstein who was forced to leave Germany because he could not agree with the Nazi conception of physics, is a citizen of the United States. [Necessary comma after *Einstein* omitted.]

## Omitting Obstructive Marks

An unnecessary mark is worse than useless. It is an interruption. For example:

Lewis's Gopher Prairie is an ugly, little country town.

No hotel, restaurant, dining room, or kitchen shall be used as a sleeping or dressing room by an employee or other person.— Cited from a North Dakota statute in Albert H. Marckwardt's *Introduction to the English Language.* [The first comma makes it appear that the law forbids any person to sleep in a North Dakota hotel.]

Students, who attend all of the off-campus games, are likely to make poor grades. [The commas make the sentence ridiculous; it seems to say that students in general attend all the off-campus games and that all students are likely to make poor grades.]

I am, accordingly, returning the policy for correction. [The commas suggest an overstressed form of *am* and break the continuity of the sentence.]

## Written vs. Oral Punctuation

The relation of structural punctuation to what has been called oral punctuation is well stated in Albert H. Marckwardt's *Introduction to the English Language* (p. 156). The qualification "in large part" is to be noted.

Punctuation is in large part a system of conventions the function of which is to assist the written language in indicating those elements of speech which cannot be conveniently set down on paper: chiefly pause, pitch, and stress. It is relevant here that the words *period, colon,* and *comma* all signified a sentence, a portion of a sentence, or a pause, long before they came to be applied to the various points of punctuation. Such points as the question mark and the period are obvious substitutes or compensations for pitch modulation; the exclamation point suggests the element of stress or volume; frequently the comma and semicolon correspond to pauses in phonation.[2]

---

[2] Copyright 1942, Oxford University Press, New York. By permission.

For example, the question marks in the following paragraphs suggest slight pauses and the rising inflection that marks interrogative meaning. Each period suggests a slight pause and the falling inflection that marks the end of a declarative group. The commas in the first paragraph, each marking the end of an adverbial beginning that would make a natural breath group in speech, correspond to brief pauses in speech and to the kind of inflection that says "Go on." The dash in the second paragraph is a suspensive mark that gives special emphasis to the long modifier beginning with *often*.

> In the first place, where do we get our knowledge of punctuation? From school textbooks. Where did the writers get their knowledge? From earlier textbooks. If we follow up this cascade, what source do we reach? John Wilson's *Treatise* of 1871.
>
> The twentieth edition of the *Treatise*, brought out three years after his death, is the great storehouse which every succeeding text-maker has pillaged without acknowledgment—often, no doubt, plundering at second or third hand, and so not even being aware whence his booty had originally come.—C. H. Ward in the *English Journal*, September 1915.

Bad punctuation may suggest awkward vocal grouping or a false stress. For example:

> A galley is a long, shallow, metal tray. [The second comma breaks a natural group *metal tray* and gives undue stress to *metal*.]
>
> He predicted that, if wages were raised, prices would have to be marked up. [The first comma suggests a useless pause and gives undue emphasis to *that*. If the sentence were read aloud according to this punctuation, *that* would take a strong form, rhyming with *hat*, instead of the appropriate weak form.]

## Punctuation a Visual System

Punctuation is primarily for the reader's eye, with only partial correspondences to the movement, stresses, and inflections of speech. One does not always stop on a punctuation mark, and there are pauses in oral reading that are not marked by punctuation in written matter. For example:

> He has lived in Cleveland, Ohio, since July, 1946. [No stop at the commas after *Cleveland, Ohio,* or *July.* The better date style *since July 1946* would represent the oral grouping more clearly.]

> Officials said that conditions have changed to such an extent since the original plan was filed that amendment of nearly every paragraph would be necessary before the securities could be approved by the Securities and Exchange Commission. [In oral reading of this sentence, boundaries between breath groups will be marked by at least two brief pauses that are not marked by punctuation.]

Though pauses and inflections in oral reading sometimes give useful hints about punctuation, they are no more a complete guide to punctuation than punctuation marks are to delivery.

### Pause Values and Weights of Punctuation Marks

The various marks have no definite pause values, and even relative values are variable. The period, though nominally a stronger stop than the colon, is likely to be less obtrusive. A mark properly placed may check the reader, or may not. Under some circumstances a comma may check the reader longer than a period in the same paragraph; a dash is likely to suspend attention more strongly than its theoretical superior the period. Other things equal, the semicolon is lighter than the period where either might be used, the comma is lighter than the semicolon, and parentheses are lighter than dashes. But there is no constant comparative rating, because the effect of a point varies with the accompanying words.

The suspensive force of a mark varies in some degree with its relative frequency. The more frequent, generally speaking, the less noticeable a point will be. This is one reason why the comma is usually the lightest of the structural marks. And the same fact of high frequency helps to explain the lightness of the period. Though the period has superior theoretical rank, either the dash or the colon may mark a junction more sharply.

It is obvious that a mark properly used gets less attention than a badly chosen or intrusive mark. A comma out of place is an annoying interruption; a semicolon or dash that gives the right signal is less prominent because it does not puzzle or annoy the reader.

### "Grammatical" and "Rhetorical" Punctuation

The old distinction between grammatical and rhetorical punctuation, based on the archaic notion that punctuation should be a complete guide to oral reading, is misleading. *All* the marks have rhetorical effects, and all of them do their part in making grammatical relations clear—not for the sake of grammar but for the sake of meaning. They are grammatical because they help to make clear the relations between sentence members, between expressions in series, between a noun and a following descriptive modifier, etc. At the same time they are rhetorical because they arc useful for clearness and emphasis. Bad punctuation, of course, is bad rhetoric.[3]

### Punctuation Is Important

The chapter on punctuation in Porter G. Perrin's *Writer's Guide and Index to English* begins with this excellent statement of the purposes and importance of punctuation:

Punctuation marks are one means of helping us get our exact meaning on the page. They do more than mark such obvious facts of lan-

---

[3] Radio script, which is aside from the purpose of this book, is said to make much use of special marks for the guidance of the reader—underscores, dashes, suspension dots, hyphens, the word *Pause,* and certain marks that printers do not use.

guage as "This is a sentence," "This is a question." They help us separate words (and thoughts) and so present them distinctly to a reader; they help group and keep together related ideas; they set off certain words for emphasis. Their use affects the tempo of writing: Too many marks may slow the reader to the point of exasperation, and too few may make him go over a passage two or three times to get its probable meaning. The writer who wishes his work to appear to the best advantage will give close attention to its punctuation.[4]

## Punctuation Is Conventional

Punctuation marks are useful because the signals they give are based on familiar custom and expectations. A writer who keeps within the not very narrow limits of accepted usage can make his meaning clear; if he transgresses these limits, his writing is likely to appear eccentric or incompetent even when the meaning can be guessed. The poor student who runs two sentences together, or inserts commas haphazard, or tries to make commas do the work of periods, or splits his sentences, betrays his ignorance of standard custom and of fundamental grammar. Such mistakes are solecisms no less serious than wrong case forms. ("Great writers" are sometimes guilty of the same sort of thing, without the freshman's excuse of inexperience. As someone has said, one use of grammar is to provide flippant writers with solecisms to commit.)

## Misleading Rules

So far as the so-called rules of punctuation represent generally accepted customs or the rules of the journal for which one is writing, the sensible thing is to be governed by them. But harmful rules are handed down in books or carried in the heads of compositors, copy editors, teachers, or writers —among them the notion that *all* adverbial sentence openers must be set off, that omission of a verb calls for an apologetic

---

[4] Revised edition, copyright 1942, Scott, Foresman & Co., Chicago. By permission.

comma, that long subjects must be set off from their predicates, that *therefore* always takes a comma or pair of commas, that a comma must never, never be used before *and* or
*but.* As a matter of fact, many adverbial openers are open;
omission of a verb seldom makes a comma necessary; the
long-subject comma is at the point of death; *therefore* is
open or punctuated according to circumstances; *and* or *but*
may be preceded by comma, semicolon, dash, or period.

### The Area of Personal Choice

Within the limits set by custom and by the corresponding
expectations of readers there is an area within which writers
must exercise personal judgment according to their intended
meaning. For example, a parenthetical group that interrupts
the straight run of a sentence may be enclosed within parentheses, commas, or dashes—of course with different rhetorical effects. A two-member compound sentence with *and*
at the junction may take a comma before the *and,* or a semicolon, a dash under some circumstances, or sometimes no
mark, according to the structure of the sentence and the
degree of distinctness the writer wishes to give the members.
To take a simple example, compare three possible groupings
of the words "Prices may be down a little next spring but
anything resembling a recession is unlikely."

> Prices may be down a little next spring, but anything re-
> sembling a recession is unlikely.

> Prices may be down a little next spring; but anything re-
> sembling a recession is unlikely.

> Prices may be down a little next spring. But anything re-
> sembling a recession is unlikely.

The comma marks the boundary least sharply. A semicolon at the junction gives the members more distinctness.
The third grouping gives the two groups the rank of sentences, with the greater prominence suggested by that rank-

ing. All three groupings are within the limits of good custom; which one is best depends on the circumstances under which the words are used. Without the context one cannot say which is best.

## Punctuation Marks Are Disjunctive

A punctuation mark groups expressions for separate notice. If the expressions ought to be fused, the separative mark is an obstruction; if they require separate attention, punctuation is useful. As a rule, a subject is not separated from its verb unless a parenthetical group or some other interrupter stands between subject and verb. Verb and complement are normally grouped together. A noun and its definer are also grouped together, as in *Mark Twain the satirist* or *the fire that swept the town.* On the other hand, punctuation is needed between noun and following descriptive modifier, after many adverbial sentence openers, between members of most compound sentences, before and after parenthetical expressions within sentences, and wherever else the meaning and relation would not be clear without disjunction.

## Consistency in Punctuation

In addition to the customs generally observed by competent writers, there are office rules set forth in the stylebooks of periodicals and book publishers. For example, the University of Chicago Press follows the style *tin, lead, and zinc,* but many newspapers and some magazines omit the comma before *and* (*tin, lead and zinc*), with occasional exceptions for the sake of easier reading. Such rules are necessary for the sake of consistency, which is one mark of good printing. Though there cannot be fixed rules for all patterns, there must be directions for the position of comma or other structural mark in relation to the closing quote, for the punctuation of certain sideheads, and for other matters in which consistency is a jewel. But good printers provide for exceptions. For example, John Benbow writes as follows:

> It should be understood that this book contains no rules which must be followed in printing the books of the Oxford University Press in America. We do not question the right of an author to spell, capitalize, and punctuate as he wishes—provided he follows consistently a recognizable system. Everyone who is connected with the production department of a publishing house knows that it is not quite so important that rules be good as that they be consistently observed. Some writers and printers will not agree with all our practices and usages; we have our own reasons for them, others may have equally good reasons for theirs. But if these (or any other) rules are followed consistently the work of author and printer will be lightened.[5]

And the University of Chicago Press makes a remark in similar vein:

> Typography, like any art, is bound by conventions and rules. Perhaps in the deference which must be paid to consistency and uniformity of style it is as confined to precept as many an exact science. Since this is a manual of practice, the apparent dogmatism in many of the prescriptions will be understandable. The publisher must decide, or at least act as if a decision had been made, in cases where scholars are still debating. Few of the rules contained in this book are absolutely inviolable. They were not devised to torment or to plague the author but to aid him in obtaining for his work the virtue of consistency.[6]

### Economy and Design

Printers set a high value on economy and good design, which are closely related. They prefer not to use a semicolon when a comma will do the work, or a comma when meaning is made clear by the sequence of the words. They have removed end punctuation from display matter such as title pages, and from centerheads, running heads, and flush side-

---

[5] John Benbow, *Manuscript & Proof*, 3d ed. Copyright 1937, Oxford University Press, New York. By permission.

[6] *A Manual of Style*, 10th ed. Copyright 1937, The University of Chicago Press, Chicago. By permission.

heads such as the one above this paragraph. They have almost completely banned such ugly and unnecessary combinations as colon with dash and comma with dash. Printers also do their best to keep from having hyphens at the ends of three successive lines, or at the end of the last line but one of a paragraph, or at the end of a page. And many of them are making successful war on the hyphen nuisance by converting hyphened compounds into solid or open forms.

## Punctuation a Part of the Writing Process

Punctuation is not the mere routine business of inserting marks in words already composed. It is part of the process of writing good paragraphs and sentences and grouping them well by suitable paragraph breaks and punctuation marks and by the omission of useless marks. If a passage calls for stiff and frequent punctuation, revision will call for better word order and perhaps condensation and lightening, with consequent changes of grouping.

Good punctuation is possible only in good writing. If sentence structure is lame or stiff, punctuation is only patchwork, helping after a fashion but also showing how bad the word pattern is. For example:

> He, in his perplexity, went to his banker for advice. [Awkward interruption between subject and verb. Rewording necessary.]
>
> The result of this generally peaceful penetration, as the Germans slyly called it, of Russia appeared in the second campaign of the war. [The parenthetical clause splits a natural group *penetration of Russia.*]

## The Standard of Usage in Punctuation

As C. H. Ward said long ago, the best authority on punctuation is the actual practice of reputable publishers, which practice makes a well defined but flexible code.

> Authors have never made the least contribution to the art. (Don't be offended by the rashness of such a sweeping negative. Ponder the

statement calmly for several months before denying it.) **No impression**
is more consistently conveyed by our *Compositions* than that we refer
to literature for the standard of punctuation in the same way that we
do for diction and syntax. "Some writers" do thus and so, we are told.
What "some writers" do is not of the least importance. The vast majority of them are following as best they can a system that other authors
never originated. . . . That system has always been devised and
amended, not by authors or professors, but by publishers.[7]

"The dozens of publishers," says Ward, "are zealous to display current literature in the most attractive and easily
understood way; they employ men whose life study has been
to know what points mean to the world, to know what modern conventions really are, to follow and conform to good
usage." [8]

What is said hereafter about standard ways of punctuating
the various patterns—sentences, members of compound sentences, modifiers, and so on—is based on careful observation
of recent practice in the better magazines and newspapers,
especially in material by staff writers. No attempt has been
made to explore the punctuation of advertisements or general literature. However interesting these may be, they are
too much a law to themselves to be taken as models of standard practice.

---

[7] Article "Punctator Gingriens": A Call to Arms, *English Journal*, September 1915.
[8] *What Is English?* (1917), p. 147. Scott, Foresman & Co., Chicago.

# CHAPTER 2

## PARAGRAPHS AND SIGNS OF PARAGRAPH RELATION

A paragraph is a unit consisting sometimes of a single sentence but more commonly of two or more sentences grouped together for the sake of clearness and proper management of emphasis. Most paragraphs are not independent units but subsidiary parts of longer compositions in which a paragraph may do introductory, developing, transitional, or concluding work, or two kinds at once. In short articles the first paragraph will in all probability be an introductory-developing paragraph; transition is likely to be managed by sentences rather than by whole paragraphs; and the last paragraph may well be a part of the development as well as the ending. Examples:

> The purpose of what follows is to tell writers the simple things they should know about preparing manuscripts for publication in book form and about the reading and handling of proofs.[1] [One-sentence introductory paragraph.]

> Yet this simple resolution, this necessary resolution, this resolution which epitomizes the very purpose for which the United Nations was created, is vetoed by the Russian delegate on the instructions of his Government. Why? Why, in the name of common sense? Surely we are entitled, in fairness, to draw the conclusion that it is because Russia does not want the searchlight of world attention directed on the Balkans, and does not care to submit the aggressive action of its Balkan satellites, whose every thought and movement it controls, to the judgment of the assembled nations of

---

[1] First paragraph of the Preface in John Benbow's *Manuscript & Proof*, 3d ed. Copyright 1937, Oxford University Press, New York. By permission.

the world.[2] [Transition managed by the beginning of the first sentence.]

Not infrequently two elements coming from different languages have combined to make a single English word. In the word *lovable*, the French suffix *-able* has been added to the native English verb *love*. *Beautiful* illustrates the opposite process, the addition of an English suffix to a French stem. Two foreign languages may furnish the elements for single English words, as in *bureaucracy*, a combination of French and Greek elements, and *asafetida*, in which Persian and Latin are joined. Words like these, composed of elements from different languages, are called *hybrids*.[3] [Developing paragraph.]

The Balkan peasant is a long-suffering but stubborn fellow, capable of fierce angers when his sullen patience snaps. Whether he can be successfully communized is a question that cannot soon be answered, but the answer will certainly determine the future of the Balkans. Meantime he holds in his hands a power greater than the power of the purse or the ballot, for in these dependencies money is about as valueless as the vote. Bread is what counts. The cartoonist who depicted a loaf of bread as the present balance of power spoke more to the point than most of the speechifiers in the General Assembly.[4] [Closing paragraph that completes the development of a four-paragraph editorial.]

## Visual Signs of the Paragraph

Paragraphs are commonly made distinct by indention of the first line and by a remainder of white space at the end of the last line.[5] Indention depths in printed matter are gov-

---

[2] *New York Times* editorial, "Challenge to the Assembly," September 17, 1947. By permission.

[3] Albert H. Marckwardt, *Introduction to the English Language*. Copyright 1942, Oxford University Press, New York. By permission.

[4] From the *New York Times*, October 10, 1947. By permission.

[5] In some publications the first paragraph of a chapter or section is not indented. If a paragraph begins with an ornament or with a large initial letter, indention is unnecessary. In the block style common in poster and advertising work and often used in business letters, white space between paragraphs marks paragraph breaks without indention. In single-spaced typewritten matter with regular indention, double spacing between paragraphs is common.

erned by office rules. First lines in typewritten matter are commonly indented five spaces.

In tabular work, where a single grammatical unit is divided into paragraphs, double indention may be necessary. For example:

Subordinate clauses are classified as follows according to their grammatical functions:

1. Substantive clauses serving as
   (a) Subjects of verbs
   (b) Appositives
   (c) Complements of verbs
2. Adjectival clauses modifying nouns or pronouns
3. Adverbial clauses, usually modifying verbs or entire sentences

In book indexes, glossaries, and reference material in which the beginnings deserve special attention, reverse indention (hanging indention) is common, with first lines flush, other lines indented. The University of Chicago Press *Manual of Style* uses regular indention in the Preface and the first 18 pages of text, but changes to reverse indention in the Rules for Composition and the Glossary of Technical Terms.

In a book containing a Glossary of Grammatical Terms one entry might appear as follows:

**Complex sentence.** A sentence containing a subordinate clause in addition to or as an integral part of the main framework.

## Paragraphing a Kind of Punctuation

A period that marks the boundary between sentences makes them more distinct than the minor units of the paragraph. A paragraph break makes larger units distinct for the same purpose—clearness and emphasis. Other things equal, a single sentence set as a paragraph is more prominent than a sentence that makes only part of a paragraph; a sequence of sentences set as a paragraph is more prominent than if they made part of a paragraph. Good paragraphing gives each group its proper weight in the context. A familiar example is the newslead paragraph—commonly but not always a single sentence—which gives the gist of the story and is therefore a natural unit that deserves prominence.

## Paragraph Length and Paragraphing

Paragraphs vary so greatly in length and structure that no simple rule for paragraphing can be given. The most important considerations are as follows:

1. It is common sense to put into a single paragraph material that ought to be seen together in rapid sequence. Otherwise the paragraph is not a clear unit. But a "one topic to a paragraph" rule is not helpful, because a topic may require development in several paragraphs.

2. For rapid or desultory reading, especially by uneducated or impatient readers, the average paragraph should be short. Trained readers can manage the longer paragraphs that are convenient when the writer is dealing with ideas that require careful statement. If the paragraphs are inconveniently long or short, the reader will have to regroup the material—if he is willing to take the trouble.

3. Paragraphing is a way of giving the parts of a composition their right degrees of distinctness. A single sentence or short sequence that deserves emphasis may take paragraph rank. Minor material should be less prominent.

4. In short pages, in narrow columns, or in large print, paragraphs should be short enough in words to keep from looking too long. This consideration is more important in posters and advertisements than in text matter.

5. It is usually convenient to make a paragraph break before an introductory or transitional sentence or after a summary. But a transition may be managed within a paragraph, and a paragraph may end with forward-looking matter that will be developed in a following passage. No general rule can be a substitute for common sense in such decisions.

**6.** In dialog, a change of speaker calls for a new paragraph unless the change is made clear by the words Question and Answer.

In his useful chapter on the forms and uses of paragraphs, Porter G. Perrin gives the following estimates of usual paragraph lengths:[6] in newspapers, usually under 75 words, 20 to 50 words being typical; in fairly popular magazines, rarely 200 words, typically 100 to 150 words; in magazines of restricted circulation, something like book paragraph length. "Books," he says, "show great variety, but as a rule paragraphs of less than 125 words would be short and paragraphs of over 250 rather long except in books intended for a special audience."

Perrin reports the following word counts in selected specimens of factual writing, sixteen paragraphs for each specimen:

| | Longest | Shortest | Average |
|---|---|---|---|
| A news story | 93 | 18 | 38 |
| Another news story | 71 | 18 | 41 |
| Article in the *Atlantic Monthly* | 141 | 65 | 95 |
| A *New Yorker* profile | 306 | 11 | 149 |
| Margaret Leach, *Reveille in Washington* | 302 | 53 | 147 |
| Chapter 3 of Perrin's *Writer's Guide and Index to English* | 439 | 25 | 137 |

### Punctuation to Exhibit Paragraph Relation

Though the relation between paragraph and paragraph is usually made clear by the wording, with no mechanical aid except the usual sentence point and paragraph break, special circumstances may make a colon, a pair of parentheses, or a dash a useful sign of paragraph relation.

If a paragraph or the last sentence of a paragraph is a peg on which following matter is hung, a colon says in effect "Read this in connection with what follows." For example:

---

[6] *Writer's Guide and Index to English,* p. 56. Copyright 1942, Scott, Foresman & Co., Chicago. By permission.

Here is the situation in brief:

The advocates of the hospital bond issue say that the city has no free clinic, no medical center, and only a third as many hospital beds as our 75,000 people need.

Opponents say . . .

Though the colon is being increasingly used in this manner after introductory words, some writers and copy editors dislike this style on the ground that the colon is stiff. As a matter of fact, most introductory sentences are punctuated with periods. But it is generally agreed that the colon is proper after words that introduce a table or a separately paragraphed quotation.

### Punctuation of Tabular Paragraphs

If the items in a series of separately paragraphed tabular items are sentences, they are usually punctuated with periods, except when question form calls for interrogation marks. If they are subordinate expressions (phrases or subordinate clauses), they need no terminal punctuation. For example:

The committee made the following recommendations:
1. Adoption of uniform traffic regulations by cities
2. Publication of summaries for laymen

Such tabular paragraphs sometimes appear with a semicolon after each item except the last and a period after the last—quite unnecessarily. The paragraph breaks make the lines of division clear.

An occasional variant of the colon after introductory words is the dash. For example:

The committee respectfully recommends—
1. That the annual meeting this year be held on the first Monday in May
2. That this meeting be public

In the above example the introductory words might well be left unpunctuated.

### Parenthetical Paragraphs

To mark a paragraph as an aside, one encloses it in parentheses, with the last period or other sentence point inside the closing parenthesis. For example, Perrin makes the following parenthetical comment at the end of Section 3a of the chapter cited. The material of the paragraph illustrates certain considerations that apply in paragraphing.

> (I had originally thought that the material of the foregoing two paragraphs would be in one, but it grew too long and so I broke it at a natural turn, *The point is* . . . This gives better emphasis and is more convenient to read. Also I feel by now that "Topic sentences" deserves a special heading as well as a separate paragraph or two. The material is growing.) [7]

If a paragraph is left incomplete—"You finish it, or watch carefully how I finish it"—one may mark that fact by using a two-em dash or suspension dots. This practice belongs to imaginative rather than to factual writing. Examples:

> In any political campaign the outs call the ins a pack of bureaucrats, petty tyrants, wasters, and tax eaters. And the ins have their names for the outs—reactionaries, hungry political gangsters, and so on. As the pot said to the kettle——

> A certain young man got a $20,000 legacy Monday, a shiny roadster and an assortment of not very blue chips Tuesday, a margin call Friday. A fool and his money . . .

Serial numbers or letters are often useful as signs of paragraph relation. A paragraph serial is usually followed by a period, less often enclosed in parentheses or followed by a closing parenthesis. Another style uses boldface serials, sepa-

---

[7] *Writer's Guide and Index to English,* p. 59. Copyright 1942, Scott, Foresman & Co., Chicago. By permission.

rated from the first word of the paragraph by space without punctuation.

### Half-paragraph Marks

The old custom of using period and dash to mark a division within a paragraph not sufficiently marked by a period is nearly obsolete. For this purpose *Newsweek* uses three spaced dots (with no sentence period) in its "Periscope," where several separate matters are grouped together in what looks like one paragraph under such a heading as "Capital Straws." For the same purpose one department of the *Wall Street Journal* uses three asterisks * * * in addition to the end punctuation of the preceding sentence.

### No Paragraph Break Before Last Line of Page

For the sake of easy reading and good page design, there should be no paragraph break before the last line of a page. This is a good rule for typed or pen manuscript as well as for print.

The following chapter, Division of Paragraph into Sentences, deals with the internal structure of paragraphs.

# DIVISION OF PARAGRAPH INTO SENTENCES

Though a single sentence may stand as a paragraph, the paragraph is more often a sequence of two or more sentences so grouped as to make clear the meaning and relation of the parts and their weights in the context. Relations within the paragraph are shown partly by connective words (*on the other hand, and, for the same reason,* etc.), partly by the structure and order of the parts, partly by reference to material in preceding or following sentences, partly by initial capitals and terminal punctuation marks.

The sentence points—period being much the most frequent—help to mark the successive steps in the progress of the paragraph, each sentence usually being a group capable of standing as a complete grammatical unit and one that ought to have the distinctness given it by a capitalized beginning and a sentence point at the end. (It will be shown in Chapter 4 that some groups capable of standing as sentences are better grouped as parts of compound sentences.)

## What Is a Sentence?

How difficult this is to answer is made clear by the great grammars, though the little grammars make short work of it. But for the purposes of writing, a simple definition is possible. A sentence is a group that properly begins with a capital (not following an interior mark such as a semicolon) and ends with a period or other terminal mark. This definition provides not only for grammatically complete sentences but also for occasional groups that lack subject or verb or both, for groups that are purposely left incomplete, and for sentences that act as pegs on which following matter is hung. As every writer knows, a *Yes* or *Perhaps* or *Why not?* or *What of it?* may stand as a sentence if the context makes such a group clear. Now and then, especially in imaginative writing, one may break a sentence off and leave the rest to the reader's imagination. More frequent than uncompleted sentences are sentences that formally introduce a following sentence or passage.

### Types of Sentences

Sentences occur in so many patterns that great variety is possible according to requirements of rhythm, emphasis, and clearness. According to the basis chosen, sentences may be classified in several ways.

1. According to structural pattern (number and kind of groups): simple, complex, or compound, with such variants as simple with tag or parenthesis, complex compound, and compound compound. (Explained in Chapter 4.)
2. According to presence or absence of the usual grammatical elements: complete or amorphous, the second kind including abridged or uncompleted sentences. (*Amorphous* is a grammatical description, not a word of abuse.)
3. According to length: short, moderately long, or long. Short sentences are good for sharp emphasis, long sentences for mass, qualification, and suspension.
4. According to meaning: declarative or interrogative, affirmative or negative, or a mixture of two of these. The sentence "That's right, isn't it?" is affirmative-negative and declarative-interrogative.
5. According to degree of suspension: periodic (suspended to the end), partly periodic, or loose. Though the elaborate periodic sentences of the 1850s are no longer in fashion, periodic sentences are very common today. (For example, the sentence "Though certain details are still to be worked out, agreement is certain" is completely periodic.) The compound sentence

(see Chapter 4), with a possible stopping place short of the end, is much less frequent in mature writing than the types that make suspension possible.

6. According to emotional tone: exclamatory or nonexclamatory. Editors and news writers today consider only a handful of sentences in every thousand exclamatory enough to take the exclamation mark, which some wit has described as the period that blew its top. "Exclamatory" is a vague word.

7. According to arrangement of the parts: subject-verb-complement, adverb-subject-verb-complement, and so on. The most frequent type begins with the grammatical subject, but adverbial beginnings are very common. Less frequent as beginnings are such connectives as *but*, the anticipatory *it* or *there*, and complements of the verb. (For relative frequencies of the various kinds of beginnings found in 1,400 sentences, see Table C in the Appendix.)

8. According to function in the passage: introductory, developing, transitional, concluding, or double-duty sentences. Topic sentences, not always necessary, do introductory work; summarizing sentences do concluding work; a sentence that makes a bridge between paragraphs or within a paragraph is a transitional sentence. Many sentences save words by doing two kinds of work.

### General Rule of Division into Sentences

Neither length nor pattern is decisive. Though it is true that rhythm is made choppy by frequent short sentences in succession, and though a long compound sentence might well be broken up, either a sentence or a sentence member may have the same structural pattern, and a short group may better deserve sentence rank than a long group.

The general principle is that a group given sentence rank by initial capital and terminal sentence point is more distinct than a group that stands as part of a sentence. If a long group does not deserve such prominence, or if a short one does, meaning and not length should determine the grouping.

If a group that is capable of standing as a sentence should stand out distinctly as an introduction or transition, as a step in the development, a summary, or a double-duty group, it should appear as a sentence. As a matter of course the writer needs to make his decisions according to the common sense of the immediate situation. For example:

> Of such a flavor was Temple's mature personality, perhaps the noblest fruit of English Epicureanism—sound, sweet, and mellow like his own peaches ripening on a sunny wall. But like those same peaches the Epicurean life was a fruit alien to the English climate, rarely to be brought by Englishmen to its genial perfection.[1] [First sentence transitional-developing. The author's sentence break is clearly better than a break marked by either comma or semicolon.]

> Any farmer will agree that the price he pays for his tractor, his automobile or his clothes is too high. Most of them will argue, too, that a carpenter at $23 a day is overpaid; certainly the farmers complain enough about the rising cost of farm labor. The farm community is all for anything to bring those prices down. But the same community is delighted with its own prices. It is up in arms at any suggestion for withdrawing the government from the commodity buying markets, or for ending farm price supports, benefit payments, etc.

> . . . . . . . . . . . . . . . . . . . . . . . . . . . . . . .

> The administration is no exception. Inflation makes it possible for Secretary Snyder to manage the debt. It gives Secretary Marshall dollars for his foreign policy. It enables the administration as a whole to point to seeming boons for farmers, for wage earners, and for such special vote-getting groups as the vets.[2] [Developing sentences throughout in the first paragraph. Second sentence displays as sentence members two groups that would be too distinct if they stood as sentences. The second paragraph begins with a transitional-introductory sentence, followed by three developing sentences in parallel form.]

---

[1] Thomas F. Mayo, *Epicurus in England*, p. 95. By the author's permission.

[2] Vermont Royster in the *Wall Street Journal*, December 2, 1947. By permission.

Communist economy is no more immune to the ravages of inflation than a capitalist or semi-Socialist one. In Russia, as in other countries, huge unproductive war-time expenditures led to a vast increase in the supply of money in relation to the supply of goods. The result was "an inflationary gap" which the Soviet government now proposes to close by drastic devaluation. Holders of cash will receive only one new ruble for ten old ones. Owners of state bonds are treated better: they will exchange their securities on a one-for-three basis. Bank depositors, who will receive one for one on the first three thousand rubles, do best of all. The chief concern of most Soviet workers will probably be the actual buying power of their incomes. Since wages, pensions, and so forth are to remain unchanged, real incomes will depend on the new unified price schedules. In the absence of more data than are at present available, it is hard to say just how the various classes will fare; those whose incomes have been sufficient to buy only what their ration cards entitled them to may be rather worse off. Bread will cost them a little less; meat, fats, sugar, vegetables, and some other items, no more. And with rationing ended, they will be able to buy as much as they can afford. On the other hand, tea, milk, fruits, textiles, and shoes—previously rationed—are to be priced above the ration level though well under that prevailing in the "commercial stores." Those who hitherto have earned enough to enable them to patronize the commercial stores may find the buying power of their incomes enhanced but that of their savings diminished. On the whole, we doubt whether devaluation will greatly alter the distribution of goods in Russia.[3] [The length of this paragraph makes advisable a separate introductory sentence and a separate concluding sentence. Six groups that might stand as sentences are assembled in three two-member compound sentences. This grouping keeps them from being separately distinct, and shows their relation more clearly.]

## Sentence Points

Declarative sentences, the most frequent type, normally take the period. Interrogative sentences, useful for informal suspension and for appeal to the reader's imagination, take the question mark. In the declarative-interrogative type

[3] Editorial in *The Nation*, December 20, 1947. By permission.

("This is yours, isn't it?"), and in a declarative sentence that ends with an interrogative quotation or quasi quotation, the character of the last group is decisive.

If the emotional or satirical tone of a declarative or interrogative sentence suggests something stronger than the period, the exclamation point is available. The strongholds of the exclamation point are fiction, advertisements, and personal letters. (Of the 2,000 sentences represented by Table A in the Appendix, only five take the exclamation mark. It is significant that the standard typewriter keyboard has no exclamation character, so that one who wants the mark must strike period, backspacer, and apostrophe.) Examples of exclamatory punctuation:

> Did toil and peril stop these hardy pioneers? Not for a moment!

> Primitive man used clubs and spears. Civilized man has machine guns and atomic bombs. What a lot of progress civilization hasn't made!

> That's an odd idea [that punctuation marks are an invention of the devil]. After all, when people started writing, they just put one word after the other; as for punctuation, the reader was on his own. Only later writers marked their copy with little dots and dashes and started to give the reader a break. And now people complain that punctuation makes reading harder! [4] [ Declarative sentence at end of paragraph punctuated with exclamation mark.]

Some authors use suspension dots to suggest meditative pauses at the ends of complete sentences. In the 2,000 sentences reported in Table A of the Appendix, there is not a single case of this usage.

A declarative sentence ending with a quoted question takes the question mark; an indirect question at the end does not call for a question mark.

---

[4] Rudolph Flesch, *The Art of Plain Talk*, p. 92, Harper & Bros., New York. By permission.

The chairman asked the witness, "While you were a government employee, did you speculate in commodities?"

The chairman asked the witness whether he had speculated in commodities.

If a sentence has declarative form but interrogative meaning, meaning is decisive.

Foreign relief exports are not inflationary? Nonsense.

At the end of a sentence in interrogative form but with declarative meaning, the period is sometimes suitable.

Will you please send me by express one dozen copies of *Webster's Collegiate Dictionary,* Fifth Edition. [Period permissible; question mark more usual.]

A sentence in interrogative form may be felt as exclamatory.

Would you believe it! [Punctuation with question mark would suggest a different meaning and inflection.]

"Has your brother traveled a lot?"

"Has he! He's been to nearly half the places on his suitcase labels."

## Sentences Left Incomplete

The fact that a sentence has been broken off, the remainder being left to the reader's imagination, is commonly marked by a double dash or suspension dots. This usage is infrequent in factual writing, though not uncommon in fiction.

## Suspensive Colon as a Sentence Point

According to a not infrequent current style, a sentence introducing a following sentence or passage takes the colon, as in the following example:

When we come to the second level of scientific explanation, we find, oddly enough, that there is also one single standard formula. The reason is simple: Since the meaning of any modern scientific fact can only be explained by the method of its discovery, and since the scientific method is the same in all branches of science, any such explanation will be the story of a scientist, or several scientists, going through the classic four stages of modern scientific method: observation, hypothesis, deduction, and experimental verification. So this type of popularization will show how a scientist got curious about certain facts, thought up a theory to explain them, devised experiments to prove the theory, and finally tested it and found that it worked. If two scientists working on the same problem can be shown, so much the better: this will make the reader appreciate not only the scientific method, but also the fact that modern science is never a one-man affair.[5] [Sentence colon after *The reason is simple.*]

Those who object to this use of the colon before another text sentence in the same paragraph feel that the more frequent practice of punctuating introductory sentences with the period is better rhetoric, because the period is less stiff and formal. When a sentence formally introduces a quotation or table, there can be no objection to the colon.

### Parenthetical Sentences

A sentence that is to be felt as an aside, a parenthetical comment, is enclosed in parentheses, with the closing parenthesis following the sentence point. (A parenthetical comment interpolated in quoted matter takes a pair of brackets.) The second sentence of this paragraph is parenthetical.

### Serials Within Paragraphs

Serial numbers or letters that mark the parts of a paragraph are commonly enclosed in parentheses. For example:

1. **Serial numbers or letters.** (a) If a section number at the beginning of a paragraph belongs to the paragraph as a whole, punctuate it with a period. (b) If numbers or letters mark divi-

---

[5] Rudolph Flesch, *The Art of Plain Talk,* p. 144f., Harper & Bros., New York. By permission.

sions within a sentence or paragraph, enclose the serials in parentheses. This paragraph illustrates the style.

According to another style, a closing parenthesis is used after each serial, thus:

> Three branches of the Indo-European family of languages are spoken by the most important language populations of the world. 1) The Germanic branch includes English, Dutch, Friesian, German, and the Scandinavian languages. 2) The Italic or Romance branch includes not only the languages of the Italian and Iberian peninsulas but also those of France, of Romania, and of Central and South America. 3) The Balto-Slavonic branch, the most important of which is Russian, also includes the languages of Poland, Czechoslovakia, and certain other countries in Europe.

## Amorphous Sentences

In order to qualify for sentence rank, an expression need not always have the usual subject and verb. This is particularly true of questions, answers to questions, exclamatory groups, and transitional expressions. The following patterns are typical: *Why, in the name of common sense? If so, what of it? So far, so good. What a definition! Perhaps so* (answer to question). Such abbreviated sentences are more likely to be useful in the more informal than in the more ceremonious kinds of writing. Examples:

> Why is this so? Probably because man knows nothing so well as man.

> Can you imagine a nine-year-old boy reading eagerly about clean muslin bags and layers of tissue paper? Or about a wife disliking one of her husband's ties? [6] [Second member of a series takes distinct rank as a sentence.]

> In Britain the same procedure holds good, except that the employer is more likely to be a public board of some kind. And a person who is looking for a job has to take work to which he may

---

[6] Rudolph Flesch, *The Art of Plain Talk*, pp. 48, 178, Harper & Bros., New York. By permission.

be assigned. In Russia the boss is an absolute state which can fine or imprison the worker if he is late or absent and send him to a concentration camp as a further disciplinary measure. All this seems to add up to the proposition that the less freedom a worker enjoys the more economic democracy prevails. Which is nonsense.[7] [*Which is nonsense,* technically a subordinate clause, takes sentence rank because it is an important step in the development of the paragraph.]

---

[7] William Henry Chamberlin in the *Wall Street Journal,* December 29, 1947. By permission.

# CHAPTER 4

## GROUPING MEMBERS OF COMPOUND SENTENCES

This chapter deals with the grouping of expressions that might stand as sentences but actually take less prominent place as parts of compound sentences. For example:

> Internal combustion engines burn the fuel in the cylinders; steam engines burn it under or around the boilers. [Two members; junction marked by semicolon without connective.]

> This is his problem, and he must find a way to solve it. [Two members; junction marked by comma and conjunction *and*. This pattern is less frequent in good writing than in speech.]

Though some authorities would say that each of these contains two sentences, it is convenient to use *sentence* in the ordinary sense and to call the parts principal clauses or sentence members—groups that might stand as sentences but do not. Such groups are also called independent clauses or main clauses. It is to be noted that the words *main, independent,* and *principal* refer not to importance for meaning but to grammatical rank, in contrast with the dependent rank of subordinate clauses. A subordinate clause that serves as subject or complement depends on a verb; a modifying subordinate clause depends on whatever it modifies. For example (subordinate clauses in italic):

**Subject:** *What he says* will be decisive.

**Complement:** I know *what he will say.* The value of a security is *what it will bring in the market.*

**Modifiers:** Please come *as soon as you can.* This is the dog *that killed the cat.*

Though the italicized clauses are important so far as meaning is concerned, they are grammatically dependent. All of them are of the "essential" kind, being necessary to structure or definition. Such clauses often carry the most important ideas in their sentences, especially if they stand at the end.

### Two Sentences, or One?

It is sometimes hard to decide whether two groups that could stand as sentences, beginning with capitals and ending with sentence points, should be so grouped. If they would be too distinct as separate sentences, they may be put together as members of a compound sentence.

When one must decide whether to combine or not, form alone is not decisive, because either a sentence or a sentence member may have the same pattern. Nor is length decisive. Though a twenty-word group is more likely to deserve sentence rank than a short group, a short group may deserve more prominence. Neither is "unity of thought" or "closeness of relation" always a clear and decisive consideration. A good sentence member has no less unity than a good sentence, and the relation between the sentences of a good paragraph is no less close than that between the members of a compound sentence. The important matter is the proper relative weight and distinctness of the groups in the passage. If two principal groups should be seen together as the two parts of one step in the paragraph, they should appear as members of one sentence. In that sense, close relation is decisive.

The following passage from a *Fortune* editorial (July 1947) carries four compound sentences, one of them with three submembers in the second part, another enclosed in parentheses as an aside:

In one sense the score is better than Mr. Churchill's dirge would seem to indicate. The American going abroad this summer (and more Americans will go than in any year since 1939) will find the face of Europe fair and winning. Travel by air has been revolutionized. The sea voyage holds all of its old allure. The ancient landfalls are still there—the Lizard, the Isle of Wight, Southampton Water, the Normandy coast, and Cherbourg breakwater. Behind these approaches life goes on. The British had a fearful winter, but the fields of England were never so green. The French lack coal and bread, but the smoke belches from their peculiar engines as of old, trains run, and the American at least will be magnificently wined and dined. "Paris, my dear, is so dull." It will be a dull American who finds it so. The Champs-Elysées glitters in the sun. The Bois is there and the spreading chestnuts. At the Flore and the Deux Magots the intellectuals still chatter, and across the way Descartes lies quiet in the Church of St.-Germain-des-Près. Along the Seine couples still stroll arm in arm. Strolling at dusk. Strolling at midnight. Click-clack. Click-clack. Was there never the tramp of German boots?

There was. For all the sameness of Europe the American knows in his heart before he goes that much has indeed changed. A vast area of Europe that was once open to the American businessman and the American tourist has to all intents and purposes vanished. Poland, the Balkans, eastern Germany are walled off. Berlin, surrounded by a hostile force, resembles nothing so much as the Shanghai International Settlement during the Japanese siege. (Be sure that your driver does not drive at night over the Russian line or you yourself may disappear!) But the creeping Russian shadow is not all that is the matter. What may well amaze the American is that the part of Germany where American and British influence have relative freedom of action has made so little recovery. The great central workshop of the Continent—the Rhine and Ruhr valleys—is slowly reverting to an age of darkness. Men, women, and children are starving. Said a British civil servant in the Ruhr recently: "I wish to God they would tell us what to do, build or destroy." [1]

## The four compound sentences are as follows:

The British had a fearful winter, but the fields of England were never so green. [Two members, junction marked by comma and *but.*]

---

[1] By permission.

The French lack coal and bread, but the smoke belches from their peculiar engines as of old, trains run, and the American at least will be magnificently wined and dined. [Two members, comma and *but* at the junction. The second member of this compound compound sentence has three submembers, with comma between first and second, comma and connective *and* between second and third.]

At the Flore and the Deux Magots the intellectuals still chatter, and across the way Descartes lies quiet in the Church of St.-Germain-des-Près. [Two members, junction marked by comma and connective.]

(Be sure that your driver does not drive at night over the Russian line or you yourself may disappear!) [Two members, junction marked by *or* without punctuation.]

## Sentence Types

The *Fortune* passage also illustrates the other two of the basic types, the simple and complex patterns.

A **simple sentence** is a one-member sentence with no subordinate clause. Four successive simple sentences are "Travel by air has been revolutionized. The sea voyage holds all of its old allure. The ancient landfalls are still there—the Lizard, the Isle of Wight, Southampton Water, the Normandy coast, and Cherbourg breakwater. Behind these approaches life goes on."

A **complex sentence** is like a simple sentence in having only one member. The difference is that a complex sentence carries at least one subordinate clause, which may be either an essential part of the framework or a loosely attached expression. Two complex sentences from the second paragraph of the *Fortune* passage, with the subordinate clauses in italic, are as follows:

A vast area of Europe *that was once open to the American businessman and the American tourist* has to all intents and purposes vanished. [Modifying clause.]

*What may well amaze the American is that the part of Germany where American and British influence have relative freedom of action has made so little recovery.* [The first subordinate clause is the grammatical subject; the second completes the linking verb *is*. The second carries the second-rank subordinate clause *where American and British influence have relative freedom of action.* Complex sentences of this kind—grammatically complex but easy to understand—are very frequent in good writing.]

A less frequent kind of complex sentence has at least one loosely attached or nonessential subordinate clause, such as the italicized groups in the following sentences:

He spent a week in Mexico City, *where he attended the opera and saw a bullfight.*

Shakespeare, *who knew theaters and audiences,* managed his openers carefully.

Though these subordinate clauses are useful for their purposes, neither one is an integral part of the framework, and neither is a definer. Instead of defining *Mexico City* and *Shakespeare,* they are descriptive clauses that require disjunctive punctuation. Writers of direct English use such clauses in strict moderation; they use essential subordinate clauses freely.

## Compound Sentences

This chapter deals with the third basic type, the **compound sentence,** the least frequent type in good current prose. Though the great majority of compound sentences are two-member sentences, there may be three or more members, and members are sometimes divided into submembers. If there are submembers, the sentence is called compound compound. If one member carries a subordinate clause, that member is complex, and the sentence as a whole is complex compound—usually but less accurately called compound complex. Examples:

France has done little, and the Russians, having exceeded all reasonable limits, are now compelled to rehabilitate a part of what they carried off. [Two members, comma and connective *and* at the junction. The two commas in the second member do not make a semicolon necessary.]

Shall it [a federal Germany] be fully integrated, as the Russian plan would have it, or shall the new Germany be an extremely loose-jointed affair, as the French insist? [Two-member complex compound sentence, with comma and *or* at the junction.]

On the staff level there should be no difficulty, for the Joint Chiefs of Staff are to be retained, though all the war commanders, Navy as well as Army, objected to this committee system when they were interviewed in wartime by a special service committee on unification. [Two members with comma and *for* at the junction; second member complex. The clause subordinated by *though* carries a second-rank subordinate clause *when they were interviewed*. . . .]

General Hodge is not a man who will swap any *quid* with the Russians without getting his full *pro quo* from them. But Syngman Rhee's idea of a crusade to recover a Korea irredenta in the North was, as American soldiers in Japan say of the Emperor, a white horse of a different color. He felt that he might do better for himself by returning to America and taking the stump; but he made the mistake of saying that General Hodge is "favoring leftists," and that the American Military Government is guilty of "efforts to build up and foster the Korean Communist Party." [2] [A complete paragraph. So far as the pattern is concerned—but not the rhetoric of the situation—the first two sentences might have appeared as a compound sentence. The last sentence is complex compound with semicolon and *but* at the junction.]

## Compound Sentences Relatively Loose

Simple and complex sentences are one-member units that offer opportunity for subordination and suspense; compound sentences are assembled sentences. Relative frequencies of the three types are noted in Table B in the Appendix for a

---

[2] The four examples are from the "Atlantic Report on the World Today" in the *Atlantic Monthly* for March 1947. By permission.

considerable sampling of current writing—about 42 per cent simple, about 45 per cent complex, only 10 per cent compound. Very few of the sentences represented in this tabulation are compound compound; some of them are complex compound—a more mature type than the plain compound sentence with simple members.

### Connectives and Punctuation Marks

In the choice or omission of punctuation marks at junctions between members of compound sentences, circumstances to be considered are the length and weight of the parts, the presence or absence of connectives and the character of whatever connectives are used, and such circumstances as the momentum of the passage, the structure of the members, and the intended meaning and the best way of signaling that meaning. It is to be noted that a short member may happen to require more distinctness than a long sentence member elsewhere in the paragraph, and that punctuation within a member does not necessarily call for a semicolon at the junction. It may or may not, according to circumstances.

Punctuation marks often used at junctions are the comma (lightest and most frequent), the indispensable semicolon, the dash, and the colon. Their uses under various circumstances are noted in the following pages.[3]

### Compound Sentences with the "Full Conjunctions"

The connectives *and, but, for, or,* and *nor* are known by the not very satisfactory names of full conjunctions or structural connectives or pure conjunctions. Whatever their name

---

[3] For the sake of completeness it must be said that once in a while in good writing suspension dots are used at junctions—very seldom in journalistic writing—and that now and then a final member is enclosed in parentheses. Question marks and exclamations are almost never used between sentence members as they were in the nineteenth century. An exception is the following pattern: What is egotism? conceit? vanity?

ought to be, they have an important bearing on punctuation. With one exception (*for*) they sometimes make punctuation unnecessary, and any of them can make good a comma that would ordinarily be unsuitable in the absence of one of these connectives. The following sentences illustrate typical groupings with the full conjunctions:

**Conjunction without punctuation.** Keep both hands on the steering wheel and do not rest your elbow in the window. . . . Smith singled and Brown then hit a home run. [In the absence of punctuation, the connective fuses the sentence members. A comma after *steering wheel* in the first example would make the members distinct.]

**Conjunction with comma.** It was a good talk, but it was rather long. . . . Smith singled, and the next three men struck out or knocked easy flies. . . . Shall we decide now, or should we wait for further information? . . . The scratch of a lion's paw is almost as deadly as his bite, for he never cleans his nails, and he always carries under them rotting meat that is rank with deadly germs.

**Conjunction with dash.** General Hodge, on the other hand, backed by the State Department, has issued a warning "directed against rightist rather than leftist groups" and against the "ill-advised propaganda that if South Korea is given a separate government it can itself unite all of Korea and solve all of the international problems"—and that looks like the end of the political career of Syngman Rhee.[4] [A complete one-sentence paragraph. The dash is more strongly disjunctive than the comma would be.]

**Conjunction with semicolon.** He willed three fourths of his property to his unmarried daughter, the remainder to his other daughter, who is married to a wealthy man; and that is what his heirs expected. . . . He was at ease and had interesting things to say; but he made the mistake of keeping the floor too long. [Semicolons are used much less often than commas before *and* or *but*.]

---

[4] From the "Atlantic Report on the World Today," *The Atlantic Monthly* for March 1947. By permission.

### Three-member Compound Sentences with One Conjunction

Writers for publications that use the A, B and C style (*tin, lead and zinc*) sometimes rush to the conclusion that the no-comma style applies to three-member compound sentences. Application of the no-comma style results in sentences like this:

> Congress passed the tax bill, the President vetoed it and the advocates of the bill were unable to override the veto.

The effect of that grouping is to fuse the second and third members of the sentence and to conceal the fact that the sentence has three and not two members. The better grouping is illustrated by the last sentence of the following passage:

> The Human Rights Commission has now been requested to do something about a king of the Bekom tribes, in the British Cameroons, who collects wives. . . . It seems that this old gentleman, the king—he is eighty—sends out scouts to the tribal huts to select young and comely candidates. The girls, with "nothing on but a necklace of large seeds," are brought, one by one, before the king, who sits on his throne with a leopard under his feet. The girl's father throws his daughter to the ground, the king steps forward and places his right foot upon her, and another wife is added to his collection of some six hundred.[5]

### Notes on the Full Conjunctions

Because the conjunction *for* might otherwise be mistaken for the preposition, punctuation is regularly necessary, usually with comma. For example:

> Franklin deserves his fame, for the undertakings he set on foot were so useful that they have outlived him a century and a half.

As a matter of course, *for* may follow a semicolon or a sentence break.

Punctuation before *but* is much more likely to be necessary than before *and*. In a tabulation of 61 two-member com-

---

[5] From an editorial in *The Nation*, December 13, 1947. By permission.

pound sentences with no punctuation at the junction (Table E in the Appendix) there are 40 with *and,* only 6 with *but.* The disjunctive character of *but* usually calls for disjunctive punctuation.

### Compound Sentences with Adverbial Connectives

Connectives not in the short list *and, but, or, for, nor* are commonly called adverbial connectives or half conjunctions. Though the distinction is to some extent arbitrary, it is true that the adverbial connectives usually call for stronger punctuation than the full conjunctions.

In relation to punctuation it is necessary to divide the adverbial connectives into two classes:

1. Those that can make (not "make" or "often make") a comma sufficient: *yet, so, only, else.*

2. Those that give punctuation so little support as to make a semicolon or a sentence break necessary: *moreover, nevertheless, nonetheless, otherwise* and *likewise, accordingly* and *therefore, also* and *besides, still* (not the adverb *still*), *similarly, now* and *then* (not the adverbs of time), *hence* (the connective, not the adverb), *consequently, however, indeed.* Unlike the full conjunctions, which always begin their groups, some of these can be embedded. For example: "I am accordingly returning your papers," "The committee has therefore disapproved the petition."

It has been correctly remarked that the use of a comma before a half conjunction (except *yet, so, only, else*) is the mark of an illiterate, slovenly, or careless style, and that *so* after a comma is avoided by careful writers.[6] Compound sentences with *so, else,* or *yet* following a comma are rare. Though *yet* might with some reason be classed as a full con-

---

[6] See Raymond D. Miller's article "Coordination and the Comma," *Publications of the Modern Language Association,* vol. 23 (1908), pp. 316–328. This study of two-member compound sentences reports findings in 16,000 pages of nineteenth century prose.

junction in company with *but*, it usually follows a sentence break. Compound sentences with *so*—a favorite pattern in crude writing—are so loose-jointed as to be seldom useful in good writing.

The traditional rule is that when the relation between two principal groups is signaled by an adverbial connective such as *accordingly* or *therefore*, a semicolon is proper. But in good current writing such connectives are seldom used in compound sentences; they usually appear at the beginnings of sentences or embedded within sentences. For example, the "Atlantic Report on the World Today" in the May 1947 *Atlantic Monthly* has not one compound sentence with an adverbial connective at the beginning of the second member, but has two sentences beginning with *Yet* and one each with *So, Further, Instead, Finally, Still, Indeed,* and *Moreover.* Four sentences have embedded adverbial connectives near their beginnings: "The labor force in the mines, therefore, has resolved itself . . .," "The Herenigde Party, however, has . . .," "It is also a province of farms and ranches . . .," "He is, moreover, obstructed and handicapped . . . ." (As might be expected, there are also sentences beginning with full connectives—nine with *But*, three with *And*, one with *For*.)

In the *Atlantic Monthly* material just cited, the beginnings *Further, Instead, Finally, Still, Indeed, Moreover* are followed by commas; the beginnings *So* and *Yet* are unpunctuated. Of the embedded modifiers, *therefore, however,* and *moreover* are enclosed in commas; *also* is not.

There is sometimes advantage in so placing adverbial connectives that they do not require commas, as in the following examples:

> Fabian had a grudge against Malvolio. He was therefore glad to join Maria's plot against him. . . . We are nevertheless willing to reconsider your plea.

## Compound Sentences Without Connectives

If word patterns and punctuation are clear, the absence of a connective in a compound sentence is a gain. Compound sentences with *and* or *but* can easily be too loose; with *hence, therefore,* or *nevertheless,* the pattern may seem stiff.

Though the semicolon is easily the favorite mark in no-conjunction compound sentences, there are circumstances that make the dash, the colon, or even the comma better. Either the dash or the colon is proper when the second member repeats or fulfills what is said in the first member. The favorite use of the colon in compound sentences is to give the signal "Promise of first member to be fulfilled in the following words." Examples with dash and colon:

> When you direct the printer to 'follow copy' it means just that —he is to set the work exactly as written, even to mistakes. But in practice there seems to be more than one degree in the literal following of copy. By some printers, 'follow copy' is taken to mean that the manuscript is to be set as it stands with no attempt to secure more consistency than it already has; other printers, if they see that the first part of the manuscript has been styled, will attempt to make the rest of it follow the style thus set, and plain blunders will often be corrected.[7]

> One thing is certain: economic cycles are as sure as death and taxes.

> We can fight inflation in two ways: we can increase production, and we can reduce our huge national debt.

In either of the last two, a dash might replace the colon. The colon is traditionally used—very infrequently in American journalistic writing—to mark the main junction in a compound compound sentence that has submembers separated by semicolons. Example of this pattern:

> The army was in desperate plight: food and other supplies were running short; soldiers were deserting; and the expected reinforce-

---

[7] John Benbow, *Manuscript & Proof.* Copyright 1937, Oxford University Press, New York. By permission.

ments did not come in. [The odds of usage greatly favor a sentence break rather than a colon junction, and comma rather than semicolon before *and*.]

## No-Conjunction Sentences with Semicolon

In compound sentences without conjunctions, semicolons are used much oftener than dashes, commas, or colons. (Of the 102 two-member compound sentences represented by the second part of Table E in the Appendix under the heading "No Connectives at Junctions," 75 mark the junctions with semicolon, 13 with colon, 9 with comma, 5 with dash.) Examples with semicolon:

The semicolon is a coordinating mark; the colon is an anticipatory mark carrying the idea "as follows."

*Father* and *mother* are not derivatives of Latin *pater* and *mater*; they are cognate words from the same Indo-European stock.

Soaking the idle rich is one thing; soaking corporations is something else.

Corporations don't pay excise taxes; they collect them for the government from you and me.

Bee lining is neither mysterious nor complicated. One takes a small covered box with a section of comb honey to an open field where asters and goldenrod hold blossoms to the sky. A bee comes to the box; after he has loaded a supply he takes off in a straight line for his tree home. He returns with friends. One watches the direction. When the next group comes back the cover is put on the box. . . .[8] [The semicolon in the third sentence is like a reduced period.]

But the government was not able to interfere, at least not in any major way. It had to let the market operate. The market performed the job. That it caused dislocation and inflicted hardship is obvious. But the government controls would have done the same. The people injured are now able to see what is ahead and to adjust themselves to it. A government bureau would have had

---

[8] From a *New York Times* editorial, September 15, 1947. By permission.

them in a state of uncertainty for months. And finally the government would have had to do just what was done; it would have had to pay a price to those who owned the grain.[9] [Nine groups that might stand as sentences. The first seven are so grouped; the last two are evidently intended to be seen together as the last step in the paragraph.]

## The Comma in No-Conjunction Compound Sentences

The so-called comma splice is like the little girl in the nursery rhyme; when it is good it is very very good, and when it is bad it is horrid. In the half-literate papers of unpromising college freshmen it is nearly always bad, and deserves the opprobrious names given it—child's error, baby comma, or false comma. But skilful writers who know what circumstances make the comma sufficient in the absence of a conjunction need not deny themselves the use of so light and swift a mark as the comma. For example, the second sentence of the following paragraph puts two closely parallel groups into a two-member compound sentence in order to let the reader see them together. The junction is marked by a comma without connective, the relation being also marked by the form of the members. The comma is better in this sentence than the semicolon that might have been used.

> The fact is that central planning has proved far more complicated than the planners imagined. Allocation of coal leads on to allocation of steel, allocation of steel puts the hand of government in almost every line of industry. In place of millions of prices directing human activity we get millions of pieces of paper. The *Papierkrieg* is not confined to Germany. It is a universal European phenomenon. All Europe resembles a great correspondence school where manufacturers and government officials solemnly write back and forth to each other. "In the old days," remarks a British textile man, "my secretary handled all government correspondence. Now we have one clerk in the firm to do nothing else." [10]

---

[9] From a *Wall Street Journal* editorial, November 7, 1947. By permission.

[10] From a *Fortune* editorial, July 1947. By permission.

The chief patterns that support the comma are as follows:

**Echo question.** That's right, isn't it? [A sentence break would suggest a different inflection and meaning: That's right. Isn't it?]

**Closely parallel form.** Some assert it, some deny it, some accept it with qualifications. . . . I came, I saw, I conquered. . . . First find the trouble, then correct it. . . . The first man up knocked a fly to centerfield, the second struck out, the third mistook his single for a two-bagger.

**Veiled subordination.** Like it or not, we have to take it. . . . I tell you frankly, I don't like it. . . . Love me, love my dog. [These might be construed as complex sentences.]

**Negative-affirmative balanced pattern.** He doesn't like it, he merely endures it. . . . He's not a person, he's an institution. [In this pattern the semicolon is more usual.]

**Verb omitted from second member.** In the First World War Italy took sides with the Allies, Turkey and Bulgaria with the Central Powers. . . . Some signed immediately, others only at the last minute. . . . In twelve months food costs in large cities had risen 31%, clothing 18%, house furnishings 17%.

**A common modifier.** The A.F.S.C. [American Friends Service Committee] has a staff of 530 people, many of them unpaid volunteers, and a 1948 operating budget of $7 million which they raise mostly from non-Quaker sources. At present they run refugee camps in both India and Pakistan, they feed and clothe Japanese and give medical service in China, they help Finns drain swamps near the Arctic Circle, they teach ABCs to Mexicans, they rebuild schools in the Tennessee mountains and houses in the Chicago slums. A highly characteristic new project is in Germany, where a dozen or so A.F.S.C. workers have probably drawn closer to the German people than any other Americans.[11] [The second sentence is a four-member compound sentence with the common modifier *At present*. This and parallel form make the commas good.]

It is important to remember that semicolons are used eight or ten times as often as commas in no-conjunction compound

---

[11] From an editorial in *Life,* January 26, 1948. By permission.

sentences, even by writers who know when the comma will serve. For unskilled writers the traditional rule is safe: "If you write a compound sentence with no conjunction, use the semicolon unless the introductory character of the first member makes the colon better."

## Compound Sentences with Amorphous Members

An expression that lacks subject or verb or both, or one that has the form of a subordinate clause, may sometimes take the rank of a sentence member. For example:

> Perhaps so, but the chances are against it. [First member amorphous.] . . . True enough, but what of it? [Both members amorphous.] . . . In general, yes; but in this case there is reasonable doubt. . . . The result: the high-tariff crowd took a beating. [Colon suitable because the second group is in apposition with the first.] . . . The directors passed the quarterly dividend and the usual December extra; whereupon the stock dropped five points. [Though the group beginning *whereupon* is technically subordinate, the semicolon gives it the effect of a sentence member.]

# CHAPTER 5

# GROUPING MODIFIERS, APPOSITIVES, AND PARENTHETICAL EXPRESSIONS

Modifiers, appositives, and the loosely attached expressions commonly described as "parenthetical" are placed together in this chapter because modifiers and appositives are grouped according to the same principle, and because loosely attached modifiers and appositives behave like parenthetical expressions and are not always distinguishable from them.

The kinds of modifiers that matter for the present purpose are (1) adjective phrases and relative clauses following the words they modify, (2) participial groups either preceding or following their nouns or pronouns, (3) adverbial expressions serving as modifiers of verbs or entire groups, and (4) adverbial-connective expressions such as *thus, however, for this reason, under these circumstances, with a few exceptions.*

## Limiting and Descriptive Modifiers

The general rule of grouping adjectival modifiers is (1) that a restrictive or defining modifier is grouped with the expression it modifies, and (2) that a descriptive, commenting modifier is set off by punctuation. Examples:

> **Limiting, defining modifiers.** A person *who revels in his own emotions* is a sentimentalist. [Telling what kind of person.] . . . This is the dog *that worried the cat that ate the rat,* etc. [Telling what particular dog and what particular cat.] . . . We have never had a big boom *that was not followed by a collapse.* . . . An author *who sends in bad copy* may expect trouble and expense. . . . A friend *I saw yesterday* gave me

the news. [Relative clause with relative omitted.] . . . Is the Republican party following Hamilton *who believed in government by a commercial aristocracy,* or Lincoln *who believed in government of the people, for the people, by the people?* [The *who* clauses tell what particular aspects of Hamilton and Lincoln are meant. Though the form suggests punctuation with commas, meaning should be decisive.] . . . The company is installing a machine *that will put some fifty men off the payroll.*

**Descriptive, commenting modifiers.** Hitler began by creating the Nazi party, *which appealed to the middle class and the army.* . . . Mr. Robert Smith, *whom you met a few days ago,* will be in town next week. . . . Wars bring boom times, *which in turn give way to depression.* . . . This house, *which was built in 1938 for $4,500,* sold yesterday for $15,750. . . . This house, *built in 1938 for $4,500,* sold yesterday, etc. . . . The resolution was referred to the Finance Committee, *which reported it favorably.* [This "forward-moving" clause has much the effect of a principal group, as if it read "And the committee reported it favorably."]

The distinction between defining and commenting modifiers is generally observed in careful American writing. (The fact that certain eccentric authors choose to ignore it is not important.)

Writers sometimes have to decide whether a modifier is intended to limit or to describe. For example, one may use or omit commas in the following according to the meaning:

I took the specimen to an expert who was able to identify it.
I took the specimen to an expert, who was able to identify it.

The new book which I am using in my introductory English Language course has many useful exercises. The new book, which I am using in my introductory English Language course, has many useful exercises.

If *an expert* and *the new book* are already definite, the modifiers will be set off; if they appear to need defining, commas will be omitted.

In direct writing, descriptive modifiers are much less frequent than unpunctuated defining modifiers. Using a descriptive modifier calls for punctuation and makes one more group for the reader to notice.

### Participial Phrases

Such phrases may be either limiting and open or descriptive and punctuated. They may have either adjectival or adverbial force, despite the usual description of participles as verbal adjectives. Examples:

**Open limiting groups.** Failure of a front tire on a car *going sixty miles an hour* may be disastrous. . . . All persons *known to have been present* will be summoned. . . . South Texas may expect *slowly rising* temperature.

**Punctuated descriptive groups.** This important report, *just released by the investigating committee,* will be printed in full in our Sunday issue. . . . The Tangier garrison, *consisting of one cavalry regiment and two regiments of infantry,* was brought to Cairo.

**Participial groups with adverbial force.** *Having no passport,* he was not permitted to land. . . . For six years he was a king in name only, *the real power being in the hands of the Regent and the Council.* . . . *All things considered,* the proposal is good. . . . *There being no unfinished business,* new business is now in order. . . . *Generally speaking,* cheap stocks are more volatile than the blue chips. . . . *Nothing preventing,* the schedule will be strictly followed. . . . *This done,* the rest should be easy.

### Adverbial Modifiers

Classification of adverbial modifiers as limiting or commenting is so uncertain that questions about their grouping are not easily reduced to rule. In general, an adverbial group immediately following its verb is closely grouped with that verb unless disjunctive punctuation is needed for clearness or emphasis. When used as sentence beginnings, some two of every three adverbial clauses and many adverbial phrases are set off. And of course an adverbial expression that is felt as an aside will take disjunctive punctuation. Examples:

**Open adverbial groups.** This is allowable *under some circumstances*. . . . *When she was good* she was very very good, and *when she was bad* she was horrid. . . . Please answer *as soon as you can*. . . . *At that time* there were no good roads. *Under the circumstances* there was nothing else to do. . . . He goes fishing *whenever he can get a day off*. . . . *Only six times in all* did he fail to make a sale. . . . *When Pope attacks* he does so with zest.

**Punctuated adverbial groups.** *There being no objection*, the minutes are approved as read. . . . *The war over*, certain government controls were no longer needed. . . . *If the President vetoes the bill*, Congress will be able to override the veto. . . . *Though everybody knew what was wrong*, nobody did anything. . . . *So far as I know*, his record is good. . . . *However hard he tried*, he made no headway until he changed his method. . . . *The sooner this order is put into effect*, the better for all concerned. . . . And *though our population is only 10 per cent greater than before the war*, our production is up more than 50 per cent. [No comma needed after *And*.] . . . *Whatever form the program takes*, it will be strongly supported. . . . Such permission can be given—*not often and not without the written consent of the Executive Committee*. [Modifier emphasized by suspensive dash.] . . . House debate on the measure will begin tomorrow, *with final vote scheduled for next Tuesday*.

Disjunctive punctuation is likely to be useful (1) if the adverbial modifier is long, (2) if it ought to stand out prominently, (3) if it is in clause form (with subject and verb) and if it stands at the beginning of the sentence. (Typical adverbial clauses begin with *although, while, if, even if, unless*.) But rules in terms of length, structure, and position are subject to important exceptions. The writer needs to decide on the spot whether an adverbial modifier should be fused with neighboring words or made distinct by punctuation.

If a punctuated adverbial clause at the beginning is shifted to the end of a sentence, punctuation is likely to be unnecessary. For example:

> Unless an exception is officially authorized, the committee must follow the rule. . . . The committee must follow the rule unless an exception is officially authorized.

As a matter of course, an adverbial clause at the end may take disjunctive punctuation for special emphasis.

## Adverbial Clauses with "Because"

If *because* begins a group that proves a preceding proposition—that is, if *for* can replace *because* without real change of meaning—the clause takes separative punctuation. If the clause tells why, it is commonly grouped with neighboring words. Examples:

> But we are not happy, because we know that we are insecure. . . . General Lee declined the appointment because he did not consider himself qualified for the work.

## Adverbial Groups Following Conjunctions

If a conjunction *and, but,* or *that* at the beginning of a sentence or sentence member is followed by an adverbial group, there are three possible groupings. The modifier may be open, or punctuated at the end, or (much less often in good current writing) punctuated at both beginning and end. Examples:

> Those who think that if we do not send food to Yugoslavia we starve its people forget that Yugoslavia conscripts an enormous standing army from men who would otherwise work on farms to produce food.[1]  [Clause beginning with *if* open.]

---

[1] Henry Hazlitt in *Newsweek*, March 31, 1947. By permission.

One well informed observer says that if the signs of the times mean anything, they mean trouble within six months. [Comma at end of the group, no comma after *that*.]

The Thomas committee this week is getting information about a strange paradox. It is hearing that, despite widespread public opinion favoring the exclusion of the American Communist party from primaries and elections, it is difficult if not impossible to satisfy that opinion by specific legislation.[2] [Punctuation at both beginning and end of the group beginning *despite widespread public opinion.*]

But, when the Soviet representatives have consented to negotiate, they have laid down impossible conditions. [Commas at beginning and end.]

The third style, with comma after the connective and another after the modifier, gives the modifier great distinctness, and often has the bad effect of stressing the connective. The second of the three patterns—no comma after the conjunction, comma at the end of the modifier—is more frequent than the no-comma style and much more frequent than the two-comma style.

### Adverbial or Adverbial-Connective Phrases at Beginning

Phrases that begin sentences are adverbial if their main work is to modify, connective if their main work is to show relation between sentence and sentence. Very often they are both adverbial and connective, as in the beginnings *On the other hand, For this reason, In view of these facts.*

In the grouping of initial adverbial or adverbial-connective phrases, there is great variety of practice. Some copy editors appear to believe that nearly all such expressions should take commas; others are more discriminating, leaving some open, punctuating others when their character, length, and weight make punctuation desirable. (Table D in the Appendix gives

---

[2] Raymond Moley in *Newsweek,* February 16, 1948. By permission.

some information about relative frequencies of open and punctuated phrases that begin sentences.)

The following specimens from the "Atlantic Report on the World Today" in the March 1947 *Atlantic Monthly,* whose editors know how to group such beginnings, illustrate the two styles:

**Set off with comma:** "In drafting the satellite treaties, former Secretary of State Byrnes could count heavily upon periodic support . . ." "Despite inevitable squabbling over some aspects of the Austrian treaty, the Big Four should accomplish this part of their task with reasonable dispatch." "As a result, the Austrian treaty will carry a specific ban . . ." "In the negotiation of the Austrian treaty, Russia accordingly holds a trump."

**Open:** "In the writing of the German peace treaty every nation in Europe is aware . . ." "Throughout Western Germany the ranks of the agitators for the doctrine of the Herrenvolk have been augmented by the return of young German prisoners of war . . ." "Last autumn the British announced a program . . ." "On January 1 there were still some 3,000,000 cases . . . in the American zone."

Adverbial openers equivalent to adverbs of time or place (*Last week, On January* 15, *In Washington, At home*) are commonly left open unless there is special reason for making them distinct. Certain other expressions used as openers (*As a matter of fact, On the other hand, In spite of this*) are open or punctuated according to the writer's or copy editor's judgment. Certain others are regularly or at least usually punctuated: *for example, more important* (followed by an appositive), *in the light of these facts, generally speaking, upon this assumption*. Examples:

For example, the hybrid word *scientist* has a Greek ending attached to a Latin stem and ending. [*For example* may also be followed by a colon.] . . . More important, the proposed tax will hurt business, upon which jobs and production depend. . . . Generally speaking, a sales tax is hard on low-income families.

As a matter of convenience, the grouping of one-word connective adverbs such as *however* and *finally* will be included below in the discussion of preliminaries, despite the fact that they are adverbial.

## Appositives Repeat Functions and Add Meaning

An appositive is a unit that repeats a grammatical function—subject, modifier, or whatever else—with some addition, limitation, or explanation of meaning. An appositive may repeat the function of a noun (his son *John*; John, *his second son*), of an adverb (later, *at 7:30*), of an adjective (negligent, *meaning culpably careless*), of a verb, or even of a principal group (My fault; *I'm sorry*). The first member of the last example is an amorphous sentence member.

## Grouping Appositives

Appositives are grouped according to the rule for adjectival modifiers. (1) A defining appositive is grouped with the expression it limits. (2) A descriptive, commenting appositive is set off by a punctuation mark or a pair of marks, according to position. This custom is generally followed in careful American printing. Examples:

**Restrictive appositives.** The legal term *due process*; the clumsy word *noncooperation*; William *the Conqueror*; my brother *Albert* and my sister *Mary*; the misunderstood saying *that the exception proves the rule*. Diaz *the ruler* was less admirable than Diaz *the liberator*.

**Descriptive, commenting appositives.** Form words (*equivalent to function words, "empty words," or morphemes*) are important signals of relation and meaning. . . . Indention—*leaving white space at the beginning of the first line of a paragraph*—is a signal to the reader. . . . His second son, *now a Harvard freshman,* is named William. . . . Five of the great tragedies are required reading: *Hamlet, Macbeth, King Lear, Othello, and Coriolanus.* . . . A great linguist has said that the real guide to good grammar, *to good English in every respect,* is to be found in the living speech. . . . *An expert accountant,* he sees more in a balance sheet than I can. [Reversed appositive, with adverbial force.]

## Punctuation Marks with Descriptive Appositives

Marks of apposition are the comma (most frequent and usually lightest), dash, colon, parentheses, very rarely brackets, sometimes suspension dots in literary writing and often in advertisements. Periods and semicolons are not marks of apposition, though there may be an appositive relation between one sentence or sentence member and another. Parentheses are used in pairs; a comma appositive or dash appositive takes one mark or a pair of marks according to position; the colon is not used in pairs. Dashes group appositives more emphatically than commas. Parentheses carry the suggestion, "This is incidental; it might have been omitted," even though the appositive is to be noticed in passing. The colon means "as follows; notice what's coming." Writers need to use good judgment in the choice of marks, because no rule could cover all the shades of meaning and emphasis the writer must take care of.

## Special Cases of Apposition

Appositives take a great variety of forms. An appositive may be a series, a quotation, an example, or what looks like the second member of a series with *or*; it may even be a sentence, a paragraph or passage, or a separately paragraphed table. Appositives are often introduced by such expressions as *that is, that is to say, for example* or *e.g., especially* or *particularly, including, such as, even,* and those pompous legalisms *namely* and *viz.* Examples:

**Series appositives.** The major Romance languages—Italian, French, Spanish, and Portuguese—are spoken by important language populations. . . . Four languages derived from Latin are spoken by important language populations—Italian,

French, Spanish, and Portuguese. . . . Verb-adverb or verb-preposition compounds (*take up, give out, lay in,* etc.) are frequent and useful. . . . The languages of the Iberian peninsula, Spanish and Portuguese, are also the languages of Latin America.

**Quotation as appositive.** His words "deliberate and malicious falsehood" made him liable for damages. . . . Article IX of our Bill of Rights is as follows: "The enumeration in the Constitution of certain rights shall not be construed to deny or disparage others retained by the people." [An appositive quotation may of course begin a new paragraph.]

**Example as an appositive.** A parade of big words such as *inexplicable, polysyllabic, incalculable,* and *indefatigable* is ridiculous. . . . Some English words (e.g. *boatswain, though*) have far more letters than sounds.

**Summarizing appositive with pickup dash.** Meeting payrolls, paying bank loans, keeping overhead down, watching inventories, making collections—these are some of the businessman's worries.

**Appositives with "of."** The City of Baltimore; the Borough of Manhattan.

**Equivalent appositive with "or."** Many function words or form words—they are the same—take weak forms in speech except when there is special reason for stressing them. [If an appositive with *or* is taken for the second member of a series, the writer has been careless.]

**Sentence, sentence member, or subordinate clause as an appositive.** It is safe to predict what he will do: he will deny every charge. . . . Prediction: Prices will go up 5 per cent before they begin to drop. . . . Result: The left-wingers took a beating. . . . His text was the familiar but mysterious saying that the meek shall inherit the earth.

**Table separately paragraphed.** English has three nasal continuants:
1. The point-gum nasal usually represented by *n*, as in *none*
2. The lip nasal that begins and ends *maim*
3. The tongue-and-palate nasal (a single sound) usually represented by *ng*, but sometimes by *n* as in *bank*

## Appositives Introduced by "Namely" or "That is"

According to an old but outmoded rule, the formula with *namely* is semicolon-*namely*-comma, with this result:

To Greece we are indebted for the three principal orders of architecture; namely, the Doric, the Ionic, and the Corinthian.

The following specimens illustrate more recent patterns:

Only one power remained at war with France, namely England.
Greek has three voices: namely, active, middle, and passive.
Transitive verbs in Greek have three voices—namely active, middle, and passive.

American writers who like any of these patterns live in a free country and are welcome to their choice. But why not leave *namely* and *viz.* to the lawyers?

Appositives introduced by *that is* or *that is to say* may be short phrases, sentence members, sentences, or whole paragraphs. Examples:

He advised his client to put half his investment fund into blue chips—that is, seasoned issues with good dividend and earnings records.

Research should be expert—that is, it requires techniques not familiar to laymen. [The appositive is a sentence member. A semicolon in place of the dash would mark the coordinate relation more clearly, the appositive relation less clearly. Meaning should decide.]

He followed a let-sleeping-dogs-lie policy. That is, he took pains to arouse no resentment, to awaken no prejudices.

If material introduced by *that is* should be very distinct, it may stand as a paragraph.

## Secondary Appositives

An appositive sometimes carries a secondary appositive. In the first example below, commas group both ranks clearly. The others require colon, dash, or a pair of dashes for the primary appositive.

His older brother, A. T. Smith, *a Houston banker,* has political ambitions. . . . The following committee has been named: James F. Roe, *President of the First National Bank;* William R. Simms, *Secretary of the Chamber of Commerce;* Robert Jones, *Chairman of the Good Roads Council.* . . . The chairman—Mr. James F. Roe, *an experienced parliamentarian and a man of good judgment* —managed the conference with great skill. . . . The conferees— Senator Vandenberg (*R., Michigan*), Senator Connally (*D., Texas*), and Mr. Marshall—agreed on a report.

## Parenthetical Expressions in Three Positions

The blanket term "parenthetical expression" applies primarily to groups that interrupt the straight run of the sentence. Such expressions are asides that are not necessary to definition or to grammatical completeness, though useful for the purpose if the writer knows his business. In good writing they are part of the thought and justify themselves by being useful.

The description "parenthetical" is also applied to loosely attached modifiers, to punctuated connective expressions, and to some expressions (*Yes, No, True*) that might be construed as amorphous sentence members.

According to position, parenthetical expressions may be called (1) preliminaries, standing at the beginning of sentences or sentence members, (2) parenthetical groups in intermediate position—commonly called parenthetical expressions without further qualification, and (3) tags or end parentheses. Punctuation marks used to enclose intermediate parenthetical expressions and to set off tags are comma, dash, and parentheses, very rarely brackets except for interpolations in quoted matter. Preliminaries usually take the comma, but sometimes dash or colon.

## Preliminaries

Parenthetical expressions that begin sentences are commonly taken to include words in direct address, interjections or hesitation words, responsives, and loosely attached connective or adverbial-connective expressions. As the line between modifying and preliminary matter is shadowy, there is some overlapping.

> **Examples.** *My dear sir,* do you mean that? . . . *Alas,* there is no explanation that really explains. . . . *Well,* there is some merit in his plea. . . . *Oh,* I suppose so. . . . *No,* there isn't any answer. . . . *Yes,* the outs have a fighting chance to get in. . . . *In the first place,* the city needs more schools. . . . *For example,* our two high schools are crowded. . . . *That is to say,* the proposed reorganization is not workable. . . . *To be sure,* a bond issue is unlikely to be voted. . . . *Generally speaking,* high-yield securities are vulnerable. . . . *However,* the argument is not quite convincing. . . . *On the contrary,* the city manager has made a fine record. . . . *Prediction:* The nomination will go to a dark horse. . . . *First question*—is the proposed tax harmful to business?

The punctuation of preliminaries gives little trouble in general, except that one may sometimes find it hard to decide whether an introductory or connective expression should be disjoined by a comma or grouped with the words that follow. Some publications solve the problem, not at all wisely, by setting off nearly all such expressions. "The best judgment of today," says C. H. Ward, "is to be sparing about pointing such modal adverbs as *indeed, perhaps, possibly,* because they are much more likely to be close modifiers in the writer's actual thought, and because if he insists on expressing himself with so many jerky asides he tires us." [3] To find a comma after every such beginning as *Next day, Last week, In New York, For the first time this year,* or *Thus* is annoying. If the preliminary is *However* or *In the hotly contested Presidential election of 1916,* the comma is useful. Ward's remark is sensible: "No expression is in itself parenthetical. There can never be any rule about what must

---

[3] *What Is English?* (1917), p. 163. Scott, Foresman & Co., Chicago.

be done with this word or that phrase; it is always a question of 'Do I wish to have this understood as parenthetical?' "

## Intermediate Parenthetical Groups

Such expressions may be of various lengths and weights and may take forms that ally them with modifiers, appositives, members of a series, or even sentence members. Of the punctuation marks used to enclose them, commas are most often used and are usually lightest, dashes most emphatic. Parentheses make the enclosed material appear incidental, though material within parentheses may be intended for special notice. (Everyone has noticed that *By the way* or *Incidentally* at the beginning of a remark really means "This is important.") It is important to remember that meaning rather than form should determine what is integral and what is parenthetical, and how distinct parenthetical matter should be. Examples:

**Parenthetical connectives.** This, *however,* is a different matter. . . . The sales tax, *on the other hand,* hits poor people severely. [Note: an embedded *therefore* or *accordingly* may be unpunctuated. Compare these: He decided, *therefore,* to abandon his claim. . . . He therefore decided to abandon his claim.]

**Parenthetical "it is said," etc.** The report, *it is said,* will be sensational. . . . This explanation, *I take it for granted,* will be accepted. . . . The committee, *it is now rumored,* will bring charges. [Compare the integral form: It is now rumored that the committee will bring charges.]

**Incidental dates, etc.** In the year of the Conquest (*1066*); the Raleigh (*N. C.*) newspapers; section 37 (*pp. 133–140*); William I (*Chapter 3*); Senator Taft (*R., Ohio*).

**Incidental series appositives.** The twin cities (*Minneapolis and St. Paul*); the community property states (*California, Texas, and certain others*). [Dashes would mark these appositives more emphatically.]

**Parenthetical descriptive clause.** This sketch, *pretty as it is,* has something lacking.

**Parenthetical groups in sentence-member form.** He says somewhere—*I cannot cite the exact words*—that Iago had a moral inferiority complex. . . . His contention (*and I can see the justice of it*) is that he was condemned on doubtful evidence. [Commas might take the place of the parentheses in the second example, with the aid of the connective *and*; they would not do in the first example.]

**Bracketed interpolation in quoted matter.** "The French King [*Louis XI*] was determined to weaken Charles of Burgundy by driving Edward from the throne."

**Parenthetical question or exclamation mark.** Thomas Kyd, 1557(?) 1595(?). Alternative form: Thomas Kyd, 1557?–1595? . . . His able (!) management saved the business from total bankruptcy. . . . His patriotic (?) motive has been loudly advertised. [Parenthetical comments such as those in the last two examples are usually feeble and clumsy.]

## Secondary Parenthesis

Parenthesis within parenthesis is rarely useful, but sometimes occurs. Within a parenthesis enclosed between dashes, commas are usual. Between parentheses, commas are usually best, though brackets are sometimes used in technical matter.

**Examples.** Beaufort in South Carolina—the name being pronounced, *it is said,* as if it were spelled Bufort—is southwest of Charleston. . . . The split infinitive and the preposition at end have been repeatedly denounced (often, *too,* by men of ability) as corrupt solecisms. . . . The Bowman Act (22 Stat. L., Ch. 4, § [*or sec.*] 4, p. 50.)

## Terminal Parentheses

Parenthetical matter at the end of a sentence is anomalous, because the end is usually a place of greater prominence than a tag deserves. But tags are sometimes useful, especially in news leads, which begin with their features. Tags are most often set off by commas, but are sometimes enclosed within parentheses or emphatically set off by dashes. Examples:

**Page references, dates.** See Section 37 (*page 123*). . . . This was mentioned in the account of inflections (*Chapter 3*). . . . This happened in the year of Queen Mary's death (*1558*).

**Words in direct address.** Your car is ready, *sir*. . . . May I make an explanation, *Mr. Chairman*?

**Second member of a series displayed as a tag.** On his birthday next month he will go on half time (*and half pay*).

**News lead with tag.** Dallas County outdistanced the rest of the nation in the rate of home building last month when 700 new family dwelling units were started, *the Bureau of Labor Statistics reported Friday*.

**Sentence member grouped as a tag.** In 1946 their average weekly wage was 107 pesos (*the peso equals about 20 cents U.S.*). . . . He got the property for $7,500 (*it isn't worth that*).

**Appositive tag set off by dash.** He strolled in at 7:30—*half an hour after the time for which he had been invited*.

**Modifier grouped as a tag.** He had fallen under the influence of Henry George and the "single tax" theory—*because the chief economic problem in his country was agrarian*.

The connectives *too, though,* and *however* sometimes appear as punctuated tags at the ends of sentences. This pattern, frequent enough in conversation, looks slipshod in serious writing. Examples:

If businessmen have things to worry about, customers have their troubles, too. [Word pattern not objectionable, but the comma gives *too* undue emphasis.] . . . He is reasonably well satisfied, though. . . . Something may be said in his favor, however.

Now and then a sentence ends with an exclamatory tag such as *alas*. Such expressions are more likely to be useful at the beginning.

# CHAPTER 6

# GROUPING COORDINATE EXPRESSIONS IN SERIES

Though parallel sentence members, sentences, or even paragraphs may be called coordinate groups in series, it is necessary to avoid duplication by limiting this chapter to the following:

1. Nouns or longer groups depending on the same verb or preposition: *Anaconda, Kennecott, and American Smelting* belong to the nonferrous group. (Subjects of the same verb.) . . . Some members of the nonferrous group are *Anaconda, Kennecott, and American Smelting.* (Complements of the same verb.) . . . He wouldn't do that for *love or money.* (Nouns depending on the same preposition.)

2. Verbs or predicates in series: The engine *sputtered, then started, then died.* . . . Bad speakers *hesitate, say "the-er" and "well-er," and look anywhere except into the eyes of their hearers.*

3. Coordinate modifiers of the same expression: *A carefully planned and well executed* job. . . . The tribe moved *north in summer, south in winter.* It must be done *now or never.*

4. Coordinate members of parenthetical or appositive groups: The terminal marks—*period, question mark, exclamation, and sometimes colon*—are signals of grouping in the paragraph. . . . This report, it is *said or at least hinted,* will be startling.

5. Coordinate connectives: *If or when* this happens; trains *to and from* Houston. (Little more need be said about connectives in series.)

## Grouping of Series With and Without Punctuation

Good series grouping makes clear the relation of parallel expressions and gives these expressions the proper degrees of distinctness. If coordinate expressions are linked by *or*, *but*, or *and* without punctuation, they make a fused series; if they are disjoined by punctuation, with or without a connective, they make a distinct series. Disjunctive punctuation is necessary in the absence of a connective, and sometimes desirable even in a two-member series with *or, and,* or *but*.

The most frequent mark of distinct series is the comma. Other series marks are semicolon and dash, with suspension dots in literary and advertising text as a variant of either comma or dash. Question marks and exclamations are so rarely used as series points that they need no further mention.

Though the comma is usually a sufficient mark so far as clear grouping goes, the semicolon may be better when the series members are long or when one member carries a comma, but not always then. Dashes are strongly suspensive and emphatic series marks, easily overworked but useful when the writer knows what he is doing. Suspension dots are a literary or advertising variant of the dash for suspensive disjunction.

A series may consist of two or more members with or without connective, or with connective between only the last two members. Example:

Alaska will be more easily defended as its population increases. This vast territory has the physical resources to support several times the number of its present inhabitants. Those who think of it as a barren, frozen wilderness fail to visualize its mild summer climate, its fertile valley soil, its wealth of fish and furs and minerals and timber. Alaska's climate is little more rugged than that of Switzerland and the Scandinavian countries, which have developed a high degree of civilization and social stability.[1] [The third sentence has a distinct series of two modifiers (*barren, frozen*) and a distinct series of three complements beginning *its mild summer climate.* The last member of this series of three contains a fused series of four: *fish and furs and minerals and timber.* The last sentence contains two specimens of fused series with connective *and.*]

## Distinct Series Without Connectives

In the absence of connectives, punctuation in a true series is necessary unless the relation is made clear by display, as it is in a table of contents. The following specimens illustrate the use of comma, semicolon, and dash to make relations clear:

This is another step in France's effort to earn more dollars, to pay her own way, to rely less on American loans and gifts.

The letters *ng* represent one sound in *long*, two sounds in *longer*.

Many persons have never noticed that they pronounce *him, to, have,* or *than* one way when the word is emphatic, another way when it should not be prominent. [Series of two: *one way . . ., another way.*]

He rode close herd on the Marshall Plan from the start. After the 16-nation conferees began their meetings in Paris last July, Lew Douglas was more often in France than in London, digging for facts, explaining Europe's needs to visiting Congressmen, always staying tactfully in the background at a time when the U. S. was officially not intervening. When the conferees had finished, he came back to the U. S. with Will Clayton to help screen Europe's requests and draft legislation for interim and long-range aid. He wrote some of the technical and financial clauses himself, flew to Washington again this month to help sell the final product to Congress.[2] [Distinct series in second and last sentences, fused series in second. A feature of *Time* style is the use of series without connective.]

[1] From an editorial in the *Dallas Morning News,* December 7, 1947. By permission.

[2] Courtesy of *Time*; Copyright *Time, Inc.*, 1947.

The Republican members voted as follows: 127 for the Greek-Turkish aid bill, 94 against; 181 for general foreign aid, 45 against; 190 in favor of granting only $200 million for foreign aid, 36 in favor of providing $350 million. [Semicolons required for clear grouping of three members that carry series commas.]

The duty of the commission is to execute the law—not to amend it. [Dash for emphatic disjunction. The comma that might replace the dash would be less emphatic.]

Economic opportunity—and necessity—underlies the huge expansion programs of the industry. [Series-parenthesis grouped with dashes.]

## Series with Connectives

In such a series as *John Adams and his son John Quincy* or *Messrs. Taft and Stassen and Dewey*, punctuation between the members is usually unnecessary. But requirements of distinctness may make punctuation advisable even between short members, and often when the members are long. (The obstinate notion that *or, and,* or *but* makes series punctuation "incorrect" has no foundation in fact.) Examples of two-member series with and without disjunctive punctuation:

**Fused series with "and."** Let us suppose that the government possessed the power to interfere and to control the market. Needing this vast amount of grain and knowing that the need would send prices of grain skyward, the government would have set up some elaborate scheme to get the grain and hold down the prices. The probabilities are that the organization designed to carry out the job would still be organizing and still be considering the specific form of its directives. The grain trade, the livestock men, the poultry men and a host of others would be in Washington pulling this way and hauling that. Mr. Luckman's experience with the poultry raisers would be multiplied many times.[3] [Examples in second, third, and fourth sentences. A series of four at the beginning of the fourth sen-

---

[3] From an editorial in the *Wall Street Journal,* November 7, 1947. By permission.

tence is a distinct series, except that the comma has been omitted before *and* according to the style the *Wall Street Journal* usually follows. The two styles *A, B, and C* and *A, B and C* will be discussed a little later.]

**Fused series with "or" and "but."** Win or lose, they have to fight it out. . . . Are they with us or against us? . . . He was beaten but not disgraced. . . . Banks will be closed on Friday but will open as usual on Saturday.

**Distinct series.** Is it the truth, or only a piece of advertising? . . . A contract signed by a child or an insane person, or by any one under duress or for the purpose of committing fraud or violating a statute, may be voided. [This example illustrates both fused and distinct series.] . . . The courses leading to the Master's degree do not make research the chief consideration, but are intended to serve as an introduction to the methods and discipline of research. . . . The cost of building will be only a little higher than it is now, but about 14 per cent higher than a year ago. . . . If you will only keep your car at home while the roads are covered with ice, you won't be a traffic hazard—or an item in the accident toll. . . . He has admitted making almost $1 million since the war by commodity dealings, but has denied ever receiving or using "inside information."

## Series of Three or More with One Conjunction

Whether it should be A, B, and C (*wheat, corn, and oats*) or A, B and C (*wheat, corn and oats*, with no comma before *and*) is a moot point that is not likely to be settled in this century. Upon the principle that whatever is done by enough of the right people is a "correct" style, either is correct. The A, B and C style is followed by most newspaper offices and by some of the better magazines. On the other hand the comma-before-*and* style is specified by many books on English composition and—what is more important—is followed by a few newspapers and certain quality magazines, and is either followed or permitted according to copy by many book publishers. The rule of the *Christian Science*

*Monitor*, which agrees with the rules of the Government Printing Office, the University of Chicago Press, and the Oxford University Press in New York, is as follows:

Use comma before "and" or "or" in a series (A, B, and C), unless last two items are closely associated (cake, pie, and peaches and cream).[4]

**Examples of the A, B, and C style.** Queen Victoria was the daughter of a German mother, the wife of a German prince, and the grandmother of the last German Kaiser. . . . Good newspaper style requires accuracy, brevity, and clearness. [For examples of the comma-before-*and* style, see any issue of *The Nation, Fortune,* the *Atlantic Monthly, Harper's Magazine,* or *The New Yorker.*]

**Examples of the A, B and C style.** The instruments of the string quartet are two violins, viola and cello. . . . He does not use coffee, tea or tobacco.

If one writes for a publication that rigidly follows the no-comma-before-*and* style, there is nothing to do but write for this style—and to refrain from writing any series that will not be reasonably clear without the comma. Fortunately some publications that usually follow the no-comma style relax the rule when the length of the series members makes the comma clearly useful. Examples from the *Wall Street Journal* (an A, B and C newspaper):

"the staid, dull, and frequently controversial Ohioan"; "resulted primarily from a record wheat crop, a heavy demand for petroleum, and a substantially greater freight volume . . ."

If the members of a series are short, the no-comma style is clear enough; if they are long, the comma before the connective makes the series clearer by showing where the last member begins. For example, the comma before *and* in the following example keeps the reader from seeing a series of three as a series of two:

---

[4] From the Stylebook of the *Christian Science Monitor.* By permission.

A traffic policeman chased the slayer nearly a block and a half, almost caught him, and then lost him in a dark alley.

The comma before *and* is clearly useful in the following specimen, in which the last series member carries a subordinate series:

Dr. Stoke said that in the Second World War the United States drained and transferred to Asia and Europe the fertility of her fields and forests, the reserves of her oil, and the deposits of her iron, coal, and copper. [Subordinate series of three in the last member.]

Where the A, B, and C style is followed, it does not apply to the names of business concerns, which fix the forms of their names: Harcourt, Brace and Company, Inc.; the Atchison, Topeka & Santa Fe Railway Company; Merrill Lynch, Pierce, Fenner & Beane.

### Beginning of Series Modifier or Appositive

If a punctuated series of modifiers or appositives depends on the same word, the beginning of that series is grouped with that word or separated from it according to the custom of single modifiers or appositives. Examples:

**Series in apposition.** The coordinating conjunctions *and, but, for, or, nor.* . . . The so-called full conjunctions listed in Chapter 4—*and, but, for, or, nor.* . . . Certain words of family relationship—*uncle, aunt, niece, nephew*—came into English from French. . . . The components of a center-fire cartridge are as follows: case, primer, powder, and bullet.

**Series modifiers.** His good work—always careful, thorough, and well planned—made him a useful employee. . . . He did a careful, thorough, and rapid piece of work.

### Punctuation or None at End of Series

The end of a series subject is ordinarily grouped with the verb unless a parenthetical expression or descriptive appositive intervenes. Examples:

> Stocks, bonds, real estate, and commodities go through price cycles. . . . Stocks, bonds, real estate, and commodities, as every one knows, go through price cycles.

But for the sake of clearness it is sometimes necessary to punctuate the end of a series subject. For example:

> The modern drama, modern fiction, even modern poetry, have increasingly emphasized the influence of heredity and environment on human nature and destiny.

A series modifier at the beginning of a sentence sometimes calls for a comma at the end of the series. For example:

> In boldness and beauty of language, in the magic of rhythm, in perception of character and motives, Shakespeare was head and shoulders above his contemporaries. . . . If the cold war gets hot, if Russian armies push on to the west, the Mediterranean becomes crucial. . . . By patience and tact, by skill in getting his employees to talk freely, and by sympathetic attention to what they had to say, he prevented what might have been a ruinous strike.

## Suspended Series

Such correlative pairs as *both . . . and, not only . . . but, not only . . . but also, not . . . but, either . . . or, neither . . . nor* suspend a series by making the reader watch for what's coming. Whether to use or to omit punctuation in such a series calls for good judgment. As a matter of course, meaning and desired degrees of distinctness rather than word patterns are decisive. Examples:

> **Fused series.** Many residents of Louisiana speak both English and French. . . . Either a certified check or a cashier's check will be accepted. . . . Neither *aunt* nor *uncle* is a native English word. . . . What he said was not so irritating as his manner. . . . The memorandum from the Collector of Internal Revenue was not a request but a demand.

> **Distinct series.** Hitler said that the United States was not fighting for England, but only trying to annex the British Empire.

. . . Many editorials follow a simple plan—first a situation, then a "What of it?" comment on the situation. . . . His proposal amounted not merely to tax relief for low-income families, extension of the community property advantage, and benefits to the aged, but to a radical change in the tax structure.

## Interrupted Series

A series member is sometimes advantageously grouped as if it were a parenthetical expression. In this case the punctuation marks make the series member uncommonly distinct. For example:

Tourists will find it a good deal easier, and sometimes cheaper, to travel in France. . . . British and American aid—and money— are being pumped into the Greek government. . . . Demands on money in banks, and on bank assets that can go into commercial loans, will be heavy during the next six months. . . . It is absurd to believe that corporations are, or can be made to be, taxpayers rather than collectors of taxes for the government. . . . They are contemplating—and some have actually arranged for—the transfer of their head offices to New Orleans and Houston.

## "Suspended Particles"

Punctuated suspended groups with prepositions or conjunctions sometimes occur, but seldom with good effect. Examples:

This is a stiff sentence that throws the emphasis on, and at the same time suggests a pause at, two unimportant function words, *on* and *at*. . . . The permission he asks for can be given only when, or perhaps it is more correct to say if, the executive committee waives a standing rule. . . . There are three reasons for this agitation for, and public acceptance of, toll roads. . . . Men who buy and sell stocks can shift readily from oil to metals, from utilities to rails, from steel to foods. They can switch their funds without buying into, or getting out of, an operating business.

Unpunctuated suspended particles are not so stiff as the punctuated specimens above. For example:

He agreed not because of but in spite of the pleas with which he was bombarded. . . . If or when the President vetoes the bill, its supporters will go into action.

## Dash in Comma Series, Comma in Semicolon Series

Though it is usual to give parallel punctuation to members of a distinct series, two exceptions need to be noted. A dash sometimes replaces the expected comma for the purpose of emphasizing the last member of a series. And in a semicolon series with *and* before the last member, a comma will usually give a clear signal. Examples:

He took big profits in the market during July and August, pyramided his funds in September—and lost his last penny in October. . . . The members of the Good Roads Committee are Messrs. J. E. White, President of the Houston Trust Company; Robert Smith, Secretary of the Chamber of Commerce, and William Jenkins, President of the Junior Chamber of Commerce. [A semicolon before *and* would be unnecessarily stiff.]

## Disguised Series

For the sake of lightness and informality, the series relation is sometimes disguised by *if, as, though,* or *plus.* Examples:

It is a fine if fanciful idea. . . . In writing as in dress and manners one must have an eye to what is in good taste. . . . It is a true though surprising conclusion. . . . The company paid thirty cents quarterly, plus extras of fifteen cents in September and December. . . . In American colloquial usage, though not in British, *mad* means angry and not insane or queer.

## False Appearance of Series

"The 120-acre, 18-hole, golf course" (from a hotel advertisement) makes it appear that *120-acre* and *18-hole* are in series with *golf course.* Other examples:

The conferees are Colonel Ashburn, President Houston, Rice Institute, and Mr. Robertson. [Though the reader would guess that Rice Institute is not an institutional member, better grouping would be "Colonel Ashburn, President Houston of Rice Institute, and Mr. Robertson."] . . . This biography is a detailed, carefully objective, study of an unhappy life. [The second comma, which obscures the relation, should be dropped.]

It is unnecessary to use commas in *five feet two inches, 3s 2d*, or *five years three months old*. And of course there is no true series in *a great naval offensive, a new brick house*, or *a good old custom. Great* describes *naval offensive, new* describes *brick house, good* describes *old custom*. In the sentence "Any coach would rather have a fast big man than a fast light man," *big man* and *light man* are unit names.

In *very very wrong, my dear dear sister*, and *the deep deep sea*, commas would be useless interruptions.

### Serials Within Sentences

Serial numbers or letters marking the members of a series are commonly enclosed in parentheses, but are sometimes grouped by single closing parentheses. Examples:

> An adverb or adverbial group may modify any one of the following: (a) an adjective, as in *very good*, (b) another adverb, as in *very little better*, (c) a verb, as in *come at once*, (d) an entire sentence, as in sentences beginning with *Probably* or *Certainly*.

> The Russians, who hobbled IRO [the International Refugee Organization] at its inception, limited its favored clients to: 1) World War II victims; 2) Spanish Republican refugees; 3) "persons considered refugees" *before* World War II.[5]

The style used in the specimen from *Life* is less common than the one followed in the first illustration, but is becoming more frequent. Whether letters or numbers are to be used in either style is a matter of taste or of office style.

### Recommendations

1. In series of three or more members with conjunction between only the last two, use the comma-before-*and* style, unless you are writing for a journal that uses the no-comma style. If you

---

[5] From an editorial in *Life*, September 29, 1947. By permission.

are writing for a journal that seldom or never allows the comma to stand before the connective, write no series that needs a comma for clearness. If the members of the series are long, the no-comma style will require the reader to regroup the words.

2. Be skeptical of the traditional rule that a semicolon is *required* in a series if any member of the series carries a comma. It may or may not be necessary. If the semicolon is needed for clearness, use it; if the comma makes the relation clear, ordinarily prefer the lighter comma.

# CHAPTER 7

## ODDS AND ENDS

The first part of this chapter has to do with the use of punctuation marks for a miscellany of purposes that may be conveniently handled in a short chapter—interruptions or hesitations; shifts of structure; suspension for special emphasis; ellipsis for concealment; marking boundaries in expressions consisting of names with titles or addresses; dates, literary references, and words of measurement; and our old friend the comma to prevent misreading. The latter part of the chapter deals with certain ghost traditions that still walk the earth.

### Interruptions or Hesitations

It was noted in Chapter 3 that a sentence left incomplete is commonly marked at the end by a two-em dash or suspension dots. Hesitations within a sentence are commonly marked by such words as *well* and *why* and by special hyphenation: "Well, there is little more to say." . . . "Why, I suppose so." . . . "He stuttered his reply: 'I-I d-don't understand.' " . . . "His favorite words were *and-uh, the-uh, well-uh.*"

### Shifts of Structure

A sudden turn is commonly marked by the dash. Examples:

It was—well, what was it? . . . When we offered these reports before, we were gratified by the response, except that—well, it was a little too enthusiastic in a few cases. . . . *Judge* and *jury, beef* and *mutton, venison* and *poultry, court* and *prison*—these are

77

some of the familiar words English has taken from French and completely naturalized.

## Suspension for Special Emphasis

Even in patterns that apparently call for no punctuation, a mark is sometimes useful for suspensive effect. One important kind of suspension for distinctness and emphasis is the custom of punctuating with comma some adverbial phrases and about two out of three adverbial clauses that begin sentences. (Some writers and copy editors are so indiscriminating as to believe that *all* beginning adverbial clauses require commas.) Examples of initial adverbial groups with suspensive comma:

> Despite an enormous increase in the cost of raw materials, the company has kept its prices reasonably low. . . . Because labor costs have risen at an alarming rate, greater use of automatic machines may be expected.

Another type of suspension is the use of the dash for special emphasis at a place where there might be no punctuation. Examples:

> They left home last Tuesday in a Cadillac and limped home today—in a rented Model A Ford. . . . He suddenly turned in his resignation—because he was tired of the office and wanted to go fishing. . . . A financial illiterate who goes into the market to pyramid $500 into $5,000 will have an interesting time—and almost certainly go broke. . . . Meredith Nicholson tells a story about a socialite who published some verses in a local newspaper and then asked a literary friend for a criticism of them. The answer was that they were creditable enough to be set to music— and played as an instrumental piece!

## Ellipsis for Concealment

Omission of letters or whole words for concealment or the pretense of concealment is sometimes managed with a long dash: liars, d——d liars, and statisticians; Mr. B——n,

Mr. ———. When dots, hyphens, or asterisks are used for this purpose, they appear to indicate the number of letters omitted. These styles have little to commend them. The style *Mr. B* is usually better than *Mr. B\*\*\*n* or *Mr. B———n.* As for profane words, publishers are less squeamish than they were a few decades ago, and are less inclined to disguise the naughtier words.

## Grouping Names with Titles, Addresses, Etc.

The following styles are customary and familiar:

**Name with address.** The Ronald Press Company, 15 East 26th Street, New York 10, N. Y. If the items appear in separate lines, end punctuation of these is unnecessary unless an abbreviation mark is called for:

> The Ronald Press Company
> 15 East 26th Street
> New York 10, N. Y.

**Name with title.** Colonel Guy S. Meloy, Commandant and Professor of Military Science and Tactics.

**Name with "Jr.," etc.** John Fox, Jr. Alternative style: John Fox Jr. Richard Hobbes II. [Whether *Jr.* shall be separated from the surname by a comma is according to family custom.]

**Series of names with addresses.** The members of the council are Dr. John P. Anderson, Chicago; Mr. Robert Smith, Cleveland; Mr. Harrison Cowles, St. Louis. [If the commas are replaced by *of*, the series will be clear with commas instead of semicolons.]

## Month-Year and Month-Day-Year Dates

The usual American styles are illustrated by the following:

In December, 1948, the club will celebrate its fiftieth anniversary. . . . The armistice that ended hostilities in the First World War became effective on November 11, 1918. [Lighter styles that are equally clear are *in December 1948* and *on the eleventh of November 1918.* Another style that is gradually gaining wider acceptance is *on 11 November 1918.*] . . . The war of 1941–1945 with Japan. [The printer will use an en dash between the limit dates, not a hyphen.] . . . Julius Caesar was assassinated in 44 B.C. . . . The reign of Augustus ended in 14 A.D.

When a month-day-year date stands within a sentence, the usual practice is to punctuate with comma after the year date: "February 29, 1948, was Sunday." But it is not uncommon to omit punctuation after the year date: "February 29, 1948 was Sunday." It is safer to use the comma.

### Hours, Minutes, and Seconds

Common styles are as follows:

> The broadcast will begin at 6:30 p.m. (or P.M.) EST.
> The bomb was detonated at 9:31:45.

The University of Chicago Press specifies small capitals for the abbreviations A.M., P.M., M. (noon), and also for B.C. and A.D.

### Numbers and Words of Measurement

Good styles are as follows: five feet two inches, or 5 ft. 2 in. where abbreviations are suitable; five shillings sixpence, or 5s 6d; ten years eight months, or 10 yrs. 8 mos.; $18,501.75; $10 million, or $10,000,000; Engine No. 138547, page 1238 (no comma in serial number).

### Comma to Prevent Misreading

As a matter of course, *all* punctuation is intended to aid reading and prevent misreading. It is necessary here only to illustrate patterns in which the omission of a comma might require the reader to go back and regroup the words.

> If he doesn't answer, a long-distance call will be necessary. [The comma makes it clear that *a long-distance call* is subject of *will be,* not object of *doesn't answer.*] . . . When Jill came tumbling after, Jack asked her, "What happened to the pail?" [The comma makes it clear that *after* is an adverb, not a preposi-

tion completed by *Jack*.] . . . When the plane came down, the landing field was empty. [Adverb *down*, not preposition.] . . . In 1948, 1785 students were registered. . . . At some points on the river, ice jams slowed up barge traffic. . . . In the same period the year before, the company sold 8,000 units. . . . To John, Smith was a hero. . . . For lack of shipping, war material was piling up at ports and warehouses. . . . From that time on, conditions gradually improved. . . . Whatever money could buy, he bought.

### Comma for Ellipsis of Verb?

Some writers remember what isn't true—that omission of a verb must be duly acknowledged and atoned for by a comma in the manner of this ancient specimen:

> Semiramis built Babylon; Dido, Carthage; and Romulus, Rome.

Omission of a verb is more likely to save a comma or to make a comma good in a pattern that might otherwise call for a semicolon. For example:

> The Southern conservatives voted with the Republican majority, the Southern liberals with the left-wing Republicans. . . . Mr. James gave $50, Mr. Smith $25, Mr. Harrison $15. [Two verbs omitted.]

The following specimen illustrates the fact that when a comma is needed for clearness at a place where a verb has been suppressed, the pattern may be clumsy:

> Wholesalers of colored margarine must pay $480; those who sell uncolored, $200.

### Comma After Long Subject?

The bad old rule that a long subject must be separated from its verb by a comma contradicts the general custom of today. (A sentence that appears to need such a comma is in all probability a candidate for revision.) Unless a par-

enthetical expression intervenes between subject and verb,
or unless a series subject is made clearer by a comma after
the last member, it is nearly always inadvisable to punctuate between subject and verb. Examples good and bad:

> An article that will not sell without advertising, probably will
> not sell with advertising. [Awkward and needless interruption.]

> Everything the farmer wants, everything he needs for himself
> and his family, depends on his market. [End of series subject
> punctuated for clearness. The second member may be called an
> appositive.]

> The notion inherent in Communism that some higher power
> can impose a set of political and economic beliefs upon individuals
> is abhorrent to Western thinking. . . . The limits of govern-
> mental power over economic life should be determined by a repre-
> sentative government, resting upon wide suffrage and vitalized by
> freedom of expression.[1] [Subjects, one of them long, grouped with
> their verbs, as they should be.]

### Interruptions After Verbs or Prepositions

Verbs or prepositions are often awkwardly and unnecessarily separated by punctuation from the words that complete them, as in the following specimens:

> Please send me by express: one copy of *Webster's New Inter-
> national Dictionary.* . . . I suggest that you mail copies of the
> report to: the secretary of the Chamber of Commerce, the presi-
> dent of each local bank, and the secretary of the Mercantile
> Association.

When the first words are in the style *Please send copies
to the following,* there is reason for the colon.

### "Inverted Clauses"

The tradition that "inverted" or "transposed" elements
need to be set off by punctuation needs to be taken with
more than one grain of salt.

---

[1] Raymond Moley in *Newsweek,* October 20, 1947. By permission.

The example of an "inverted clause" given in an old book on punctuation (1886) reads as follows: "To obtain an education, he was willing to make sacrifices." The theory underlying the rule is presumably that an adverbial expression normally follows its verb; but adverbial expressions modifying verbs or whole sentences may stand in so many positions—at beginning, at end, before the verb, or between the parts of a phrasal verb—that normal position is not a useful conception. The best explanation of the comma after an adverbial expression at the beginning of the sentence, if there is a comma, is that distinct grouping of the adverbial modifier makes the sentence easier to read.

It is true, of course, that initial groups carrying infinitives are commonly set off—*To illustrate, To begin with, To name only one person, In order to survive*. But there are occasional exceptions that call for good judgment of what is best under the immediate circumstances. Examples of infinitive phrases (some call them clauses) standing at the beginning with or without punctuation:

> To get a Series E bond redeemed, the owner or co-owner has only to go to a bank where he is known. . . . In order to meet his obligations he had to sell much of his property.

> To maintain harmony throughout a book it is necessary that the size and style of the type used in the body of the book and that selected for chapter titles, headings, title-pages, and half-title pages be harmonious, and that equivalent headings be treated uniformly.[2]

> To save Europe from regimentation and communism we are asked to out-regiment Europe here at home. . . . To get that done without wrecking our economy, we must put the brakes on inflation.

If a punctuated adverbial group is shifted from the beginning to the end of a sentence, the comma is usually dropped.

[2] *A Manual of Style,* the University of Chicago Press, Chicago. By permission.

Compare the following:

> To find a new Marine Corps commandant to succeed General Vandegrift, the President dug deep into the rank list. . . . The President dug deep into the rank list to find a suitable successor to General Vandegrift.

In certain inverted patterns—subject after verb, subject embedded within the verb, complement at the beginning—no one thinks of punctuating to mark the inversion. For example:

> On the payroll today are more than 1,200 disabled or partially disabled veterans. . . . In this house lived General Sam Houston. . . . First to recover his voice was the chairman. . . . Not once has he admitted any wrongdoing. . . . Through this one center are routed all telegrams to and from Louisiana and Texas. . . . Behind this declining profit margin is the sharp rise in cost of materials. . . . Never in recent history had a high officer suffered such disgrace. . . . To a federal office in California recently came two income returns from the same person.

# CHAPTER 8

## THE INDIVIDUAL STRUCTURAL MARKS

Chapters 2–7 have dealt with punctuation according to the general purposes of marking paragraph relations, grouping sentences in their paragraphs, and so on. This chapter, necessarily repeating in a new order the more important material of earlier chapters, takes up the structural marks one by one—period, question mark, exclamation, comma, semicolon, dash, colon, parentheses, suspension dots, and brackets.

Because an account of quotation marks in this chapter would merely repeat or condense the material of Chapter 9 below, nothing will be said about these except in relation to the other marks. For a like reason this chapter has no sections on the apostrophe, the two kinds of hyphens, or the abbreviation period. (See Chapters 10 and 11.)

The purpose of this chapter is to set forth the character and uses of the various structural marks, with some information about their relative frequencies.

### THE PERIOD

With the exception of the comma, the period is used oftener than any other structural mark, and oftener in comparison with the comma than a generation ago. The fact that the period has gained on the comma indicates that sentences in good American writing have become somewhat lighter. (For figures on relative frequencies in 1917–1918 and 1947, see Table A in the Appendix.)

Though the period theoretically outweighs all other marks except the other terminal points, its frequency and its relative lack of suspensive quality make it a light and rapid mark. It is less formal than the colon that sometimes ends an introductory sentence.

The period as a decimal point and the centered period used in decorative printing and in dictionary entries needs no further mention. Groups of periods, usually of three, are briefly discussed in this chapter under the heading "Suspension Dots"; the same marks used as signs of omission from quoted matter belong to Chapter 9 below. In text matter the period has the following uses:

1. **As a full stop** at the end of a sentence that is not to be marked as exclamatory, interrogative, or unfinished. (As defined in relation to punctuation, a sentence is a group that is given sentence rank by initial capital and a terminal mark.)

   The fact that most sentences take the period is illustrated by the figures in Table A of the Appendix, representing 2,000 sentences from 20 writers or editorial departments: 1,930 periods, 59 question marks, 5 exclamations, 6 colons. (The figures are for sentence points. Colons are so counted only when followed by text matter—not quotations or lists—beginning with capitals.) Even introductory sentences are nearly always punctuated with the period and not with the anticipatory colon.

   Though declarative form usually calls for the period, special meaning or the desire for unusual emphasis may suggest the use of question mark or exclamation. For example:

   You are ready? I don't believe it. . . . Watch television grow!

2. **At the end of a run-in sidehead** that is not an integral part of the first sentence of its paragraph. The boldface sidehead just used is grouped with the following words. In the following example it is not.

   **Run-in sideheads.** Punctuate these with period if they are separate units. If a sidehead makes part of the first sentence of the paragraph, punctuate it or leave it open according to circumstances. [Some publications use colon or period with dash for nonintegral sideheads.]

3. **Between a quotation and a run-in credit,** customary punctuation is period with dash. For example:

> "The division of words at the ends of lines is always undesirable, but many cases occur where such divisions are unavoidable. Certain rules governing divisions should never be broken, while others are desirable but may be broken when good spacing demands it."—University of Chicago Press, *A Manual of Style,* p. 113.[1]

4. **Period leaders** are often used to guide the eye across the page, as in tables of contents and other tabular lists. They look better than the hyphen leaders sometimes used.

5. **Section numbers at the beginning of paragraphs** are commonly followed by periods. According to other styles, such section numbers are enclosed in parentheses or followed by a closing parenthesis. Examples:

> 1. The makers of a tax law should consider its probable effect on business.
>
> (1) The makers of a tax law should consider . . .
> 1) The makers of a tax law . . .

Periods are omitted from the ends of centerheads, from items on title pages and copyright pages, and from lines in other kinds of display matter. (This does not apply to abbreviation periods.)

### Period with Other Marks

The sentence period does not enter into combination with question or exclamation mark, colon, semicolon, or comma. Though some publishers use period with dash to set off run-in sideheads and credits, the period-dash combination for other purposes has gone out of use almost entirely. For the use of period with end parenthesis, see the section on parentheses in this chapter. With a closing quotation mark, the almost invariable American rule is to put the period inside the quote.

---

[1] By permission.

If an abbreviation period is used at the end of the last word of a sentence, it also serves as the terminal mark.

## THE QUESTION MARK

The question mark is relatively infrequent because declarative sentences in written matter greatly outnumber questions. Table A in the Appendix reports only 59 question marks in 2,000 sentences, as against 1,930 periods. Though sometimes useful for the sake of suspensive force and an appeal to the reader's imagination, question sentences can easily be overworked. On this point Porter G. Perrin remarks:

Questions are useful, if sparingly used, to focus the reader's attention, either to introduce a change in subject . . . or to emphasize by the change in sentence movement an important point. . . . Occasionally a question makes an effective opening for a paper, but it should be a genuine question, leading to the subject, and not a general one concocted just "to get attention." [2]

The question mark has the following uses:

1. **To mark the end of an interrogative sentence or of a declarative sentence that ends with an interrogative quotation.** Example of the second use (question mark within the closing quote):

   He asked a pertinent question—"What are you being asked to join?"

2. **At the end of an interrogative parenthesis** that is grouped with dashes or parentheses (not with commas). Examples:

   He told me—did he really mean it?—that buyers of these bonds take no risk. . . . He is reported to have grown in favor (really?) since the party convention.

---

[2] From *Writer's Guide and Index to English,* p. 682 f. Copyright 1942, Scott, Foresman & Co., Chicago. By permission.

3. Alone or within parentheses or brackets (properly brackets if interpolated in quoted matter) **to mark a figure, date, or other expression as doubtful, or to indicate a gap in the information:**

> In the year of Chaucer's birth (1340?); Geoffrey Chaucer (1340?–1400); George Alsop (1638–?); Thomas Kyd, born in 1557 (?); Thomas Kyd (1557?–1595?).

A question mark enclosed in parentheses by way of ironical commentary is usually crude: "His kind (?) interest in my personal affairs." As a series mark or the mark of a boundary between sentence members, the question mark belongs to literature, not to journalistic writing.

### Question Mark in Combination

The question mark is seldom used with marks other than closing quotes, suspension dots, and parenthetical dashes, parentheses, or brackets. The question mark precedes an end quote if the quoted matter is a question; otherwise it follows the quote. For example:

> The chairman asked the witness, "Are you reporting what you actually saw?" . . . Did he use the words "criminally negligent"?

A question mark intended to point a parenthetical group precedes the closing dash, parenthesis, or bracket. But if the question mark belongs to a larger group that ends with an expression enclosed in parentheses, the question mark follows the closing parenthesis, thus:

> Does he mean the Second Republic (1848)?

## THE EXCLAMATION

The exclamation mark has been variously called the note of admiration, the shriek of surprise, the astonisher or paralyzer, the period that blew its top. Its strongholds are adver-

tisements, plays and stories, and the more excited kind of
personal letters. Table A in the Appendix reports only 5
sentences in 2,000 ending with exclamations, and not one
exclamation within a sentence. In good editorial writing the
"note of admiration" is likely to be satirical. Temperance in
the use of exclamations is doubtless aided by the fact that
the standard typewriter keyboard has no exclamation character. One has to make it by striking period, backspacer,
and apostrophe—more trouble than the mark is likely to be
worth. The exclamation has the following uses:

1. **As a terminal point,** marking the end of a sentence or quotation. The group so marked may be in exclamatory form
("What a fine opportunity for a young man!") or in either
declarative or question form. Question and exclamation marks
are sometimes close alternatives, as in the forms "Isn't it a
mess?" and "Isn't it a mess!" Either pointing calls on the
reader to estimate the situation.

2. **Now and then within a sentence or at the end of a parenthetical sentence to mark a group as exclamatory.** For
example:

    In the second place, let us agree not to blame any single class
    for this inflation. Those who have gained the most in comparison
    with their prewar share of the national income, the farmers, have
    also performed prodigies of production at a time when the whole
    world depends on them. (Would that it were equally possible
    to bribe the weather!) So let's not look for scapegoats in this
    crisis. . . .[3]

3. Seldom in good writing, **as a parenthetical note of surprise or
irony.** This kind of commentary is usually crude: "His
friendly criticism (!) was not helpful." If such an interpolation is put into quoted matter, it should be enclosed in brackets.
One exception is that the commentary *sic* (meaning "That is
the way he words it") is often enclosed in parentheses.

---

[3] From an editorial in *Life,* December 29, 1947. By permission.

In exclamatory compound sentences, the usual rule is to save the exclamation for the end.

Interjections that begin sentences (*Alas, Ah, Dear me,* and so on) are usually followed by commas, not exclamations. The interjection *O* is regularly open.

### Exclamation Mark with Other Points

The exclamation may occur with marks of ellipsis, with suspension dots, before the second of a pair of parenthetical marks (dashes, parentheses, or brackets), sometimes with a dash that is not one of a pair; practically never with colon, semicolon, or comma. Ellipsis dots, suspension dots, or the dash may precede or follow according to circumstances. With the second of a pair of parenthetical points, it precedes if intended to mark the parenthetical group, but follows if it marks the exclamatory character of a longer group containing the parenthesis. With a closing quote the exclamation precedes or follows according to the meaning, thus:

> His comment was sharp: "What a mess you have made of it!"
> . . . He described himself as an "exterminating engineer"!

If a sentence ends with a quotation pointed with the exclamation, that mark serves also as the sentence point.

## THE COMMA

The comma is the least specialized of all points and therefore the most elusive. Generally speaking, it is the lightest mark for the following purposes: (1) marking junctions between sentence members, (2) separating members of punctuated series, (3) setting off parenthetical expressions, descriptive modifiers, and loosely attached appositives, (4) marking interruption or resumption of quotations, and (5) suspension for special emphasis. In its various uses the comma competes with the sentence points, the semicolon, the colon, and parentheses. In a particular case there may be no reasonable doubt as to the choice; but a given form and length of words may admit of a choice that can be made only in the light of such a consideration as the importance of a group in its paragraph.

Unlike the period, question mark, exclamation, colon, dash, and parentheses, the comma has no clear special quality save for its comparative lightness. It is not a terminal point like the period, a specialized coordinating mark like the semicolon, or an anticipatory mark like the colon. Even the dash, which comes nearest the comma in variety of uses, has a characteristic quality, and all the points except the dash have a much more limited number of uses. The comma may be used alone or in pairs; it may stand between coordinate expressions or may separate expressions of different grammatical rank; it may set off a group for emphasis or clearness even when the grammatical relation is close.

### The Most Frequent of the Internal Marks

In the 2,000 sentences represented by Table A in the Appendix, totals of punctuation marks within sentences run as follows: commas 1,929, dashes 173, parentheses 88 (44 pairs), semicolons 66, colons 53. The comma is more than eleven times as frequent as its nearest competitor the dash. The 1,929 commas almost equal the 1,930 periods, and make nearly 44 per cent of all the structural marks, sentence points included. It is worth noting that in the last thirty years or so the period has gained on the comma in frequency—a sign that the average sentence has become a little less elaborate. (See comment on Table A in the Appendix.)

The great frequency of the comma is not by any means an argument for liberal or careless use. Light as it is in comparison with other marks, the comma is suspensive and disjunctive, and can make writing awkward even when the meaning is not obscure. The effect of too liberal use of the comma is observable in the following sentence from an old book on punctuation:

> As a sentence may contain the four principal marks (comma, semicolon, colon, and period) and, in addition, one or more of the other marks, a writer courts failure if, in treating the difficult art of punctuation, he deals with the marks separately, beginning, as all writers, myself included, have hitherto done, with the comma, the most difficult mark to understand, and proceeding, one at a time, with the other marks.

And a comma out of place may distort the meaning. For example, Marckwardt (*Introduction to the English Language,* page 157) cites a Michigan statute providing that "every railroad corporation shall provide a uniform, hat or cap and a distinguishing badge" for each conductor, brakeman, or other employee dealing with the public. Did the makers of the statute mean that trainmen were to be provided with (1) uniform, (2) headgear, and (3) badge, or merely with (1) uniform headgear and (2) distinguishing badge?

The comma has the following uses, for most of which there are alternative marks. With minor exceptions the comma is the lightest and most colorless mark for each of these uses.

1. **Marking junctions in compound sentences,** especially when the junction is also marked by *but* or *and.* A sampling of 400 two-member compound sentences reported in Table E of the Appendix gives the following frequencies:

> Before *and*: no mark 40, comma 93, semicolon 22, dash 12.
> Before *but*: no mark 6, comma 66, semicolon 22, dash 1.

The same table lists 16 compound sentences in which a comma precedes *for,* and one case each in which it precedes *nor, so,* and *yet.* Before *so* or *yet* a sentence break is more usual.

Though there is apparently an increasing tendency to omit punctuation in compound sentences with *and* (to a less extent with the disjunctive *but*), it is still true that the great majority of compound sentences with connectives mark the junctions with punctuation. (The notion that *and* or *but* makes punctuation "incorrect" has no foundation in fact. Some of our journalists could improve their writing by using more commas between sentence members and fewer after introductory adverbial or connective phrases.)

In compound sentences with no connectives at the junctions, the comma needs careful handling. It is used much less often than the semicolon. (For circumstances that make the comma suitable, see Chapter 4.) The following specimens make good use of the comma without connective:

> According to Mark Twain, "Jewish persecution is not a religious passion, it is a business passion." . . . In Russia the state is everything, the individual is nothing. . . . Shortages still remained, demand still was high.

> Words are continually being added to the general stock of the English language, other words are used in new senses, words drop out of use, spellings and pronunciations change.[4] [Beginning of a paragraph.]

> They were the only survivors. In the floating wreckage, dotted with empty Mae Wests . . . five bodies were recovered, a sixth sank just as the *Hermes* came alongside.[5]

2. **To group descriptive modifiers or appositives and parenthetical expressions.** This is one of the most important and frequent uses of the comma, which is usually lighter than the other marks used for the same purpose. Examples:

> Other things equal, familiar words are best. . . . However costly, a strong air force is a necessity. . . . Mr. Howard's book, published only three months ago, is being reprinted. . . . The report, now in press, will be released next month. . . . His new

---

[4] Porter G. Perrin, *Writer's Guide and Index to English,* p. 197. Copyright 1942, Scott, Foresman & Co., Chicago. By permission.

[5] Courtesy of *Time;* Copyright *Time, Inc.,* 1947.

house, which cost $20,000, could have been built ten years ago for $9,000. . . . John Quincy Adams, son of John Adams, was the sixth President. . . . Mr. Chairman, I rise to a point of order. . . . The last speaker, bless his heart, kept the floor only two minutes. . . . Alas, the good news comes too late. . . . That, I think, is all I need say.

3. **As a series mark,** making the coordinate relation clear in the absence of connectives, and sometimes useful with connectives for the sake of distinctness. Examples:

Among the persons and institutions who are hurt by inflation are pensioners, landlords, salaried men, retired persons who live on invested capital, and life insurance companies. [The comma before *and* saves misreading. The A, B and C style would be unfortunate here.]

There will be revenue enough for a sizable reduction of the huge national debt, and perhaps also for some tax relief. [Distinct series of two with *and*.]

Far too many business executives expect overmuch from subordinates, have too little patience with them. . . . One invaluable qualification of a superior is ability to teach, to train younger men, to inspire them rather than depress them, to inculcate self-confidence, not to shake their self-confidence.[6] [Series without connectives.]

Denver-born George Acheson Jr., 50, entered the State Department 27 years ago as a student interpreter at the Peiping Legation, had specialized in Far Eastern affairs ever since. As second secretary of the Nanking Embassy, he was aboard the gunboat *Panay* when it was bombed and sunk by the Japanese in 1937. Two years later he was recalled to Washington for a stint on State's Far Eastern desk, returned to China as embassy counselor in Chungking in 1943.[7] [An entire paragraph. Series without conjunctions— a characteristic feature of *Time* style.]

4. **For suspension and distinctness, or to prevent misreading, where the grammatical relation is close.** Though this use of the comma overlaps series punctuation and the grouping of

---

[6] From an editorial in *Forbes Magazine of Business,* January 15, 1948. By permission.
[7] Courtesy of *Time;* Copyright *Time, Inc.,* 1947.

modifiers, it is mentioned separately because the comma may be not so much a sign of grammatical relation as a means of distinctness. Adverbial clauses that begin sentences are commonly (not always) set off with commas, because such openers should usually be distinct. A good many introductory adverbial or adverbial-connective phrases are also set off—far too many in certain periodicals that otherwise show good judgment in punctuation. (See Table D in the Appendix.) And a comma before *or, and,* or *but* in a two-member series may be called a suspensive mark. Examples:

Though he had to drive in freezing rain at 14 above, he managed to get through safely. . . . In school, or anywhere else, one should strive for honors. . . . As a result of this agreement, exports to Canada are free from controls, though American exports to other countries are limited by government export regulations. . . . Though American exports to most countries are limited by export regulations, exports to Canada are free from controls.

As a general rule, a comma is not useful between subject and verb or between verb and object. Obvious exceptions are that a parenthetical expression or other interrupter (with two marks to set it off) may intervene between subject and verb, and that the end of a series subject should sometimes be marked by a comma for the sake of clearness.

5. **For clearness or according to convention in various expressions:**

**Names with addresses or titles.** Charles E. Ryan, General Manager; The National Bank of Commerce, Houston, Texas; Ray K. Daily, M.D., F.A.C.S.; James R. Pierce, Jr. (or James R. Pierce Jr.); Adams, John Quincy (index style).

**Dates.** On December 7, 1941; in December, 1941. [Alternative styles: on the seventh of December 1941; on 7 December 1941; in December 1941.]

**Figures.** $19,785; 1,345 persons. [Serial numbers omit commas: engine No. 123785, page 1148.]

**Complimentary close.** Very truly yours,
Robert E. Johnson

Before the abbreviation *etc.* the comma is held by some authorities to be necessary. Though the rule is illogical unless exceptions are permitted, it has the weight of usage. Though the comma is regularly used in some offices after the abbreviations *e.g.* and *s.v.,* the open style is clear and of course lighter. Examples with commas omitted:

> Some hybrid words—e.g. the Latin-Greek *scientist* and the French-English *beautiful*—have been thoroughly naturalized. . . . See *Webster's New International* Dictionary, s.v. **compound.**

For the use of the comma before quotations or at places where quotations are broken or resumed, see Chapter 9.

### The Comma with Other Marks

The comma rarely combines with other marks, except that it may immediately follow a closing parenthesis or bracket or immediately precede a closing quote. (A comma used before an opening quote is separated from it by space. The comma-dash combination, once common, belongs to history.)

## THE SEMICOLON

The useful and unjustly maligned semicolon is the most clearly specialized balancing and coordinating mark. Though other marks are used between contrasted expressions or groups in series, no other mark is so clearly specialized. The semicolon is not a general-purpose mark like the comma, a parenthetical point like comma or dash, or a formal mark of anticipation like the colon. It is occasionally used before an appositive, or between noun and modifier, but in these cases with the suggestion that the groups are coordinate. As a series mark the semicolon competes with but commonly yields to the lighter comma. Between groups that might stand as sentences, it competes with comma, colon, dash, and period, for there is often a close choice between letting two groups stand as sentences or using a semicolon between them. For this reason the semicolon has been called a reduced period or the short-sentence mortar.

There is an obstinate notion that the semicolon is a stiff and formal mark that ought to be seldom used. With stiff wording it is stiff; with easy wording it is light and swift. It is actually used by good current writers today, and might well be used oftener if our writers would take the trouble to drop some of their *and*'s and *but*'s and use patterns that take semicolon and no conjunction.

Some of the prejudice against the semicolon has come from association with awkward patterns like the following. The first is a specimen from an old book on punctuation. The second is a schoolroom fossil that is rarely matched in respectable current writing.

> Philosophers assert, that Nature is unlimited in her operations; that she has inexhaustible treasures in reserve; that knowledge will always be progressive; and that all future generations will continue to make discoveries.

> He filed his application ten days late; therefore, he was not considered.

The trouble is not with the semicolon but with the stiff wording.

Table A in the Appendix reports only 66 semicolons in 2,000 sentences, as compared with 173 dashes and 1,929 commas. The low frequency of the semicolon is not a good measure of its usefulness.

The semicolon has the following uses:

1. **As a reduced period,** marking junctions of groups that would be too light if separated by comma and too distinct or too formally marked if separated by colon, dash, or a terminal mark. For example:

Buy at the bottom; sell at the top. But what is the bottom, and what is the top?

Good English means more than "correct" English; it means easy, clear, expressive, appropriate English.

Fabian assiduity is still turning out splendid plans. Cripps produced a beauty only last month for increasing exports; but as the London *Economist* pointed out, it omits completely the question of "motive power"—*i.e.*, incentives for human effort, which is the No. 1 problem in Britain today.[8]

The [British] government is reluctant to resort to compulsions; it hopes that voluntary restraint and self-discipline will save it from direct interference with collective bargaining. But the margin between economic salvation and a financial crash is a harrowing one. On the one hand, British production is rising, exports are expanding, and the over-supply of money is being curtailed by fiscal measures; on the other, the gap between foreign income and foreign outgo remains perilously wide.[9] [The first member of the last sentence carries three submembers, junctions marked with commas; main junction marked by semicolon.]

What mark should be used in a given case—comma or semicolon, semicolon or period—will depend only in part on the length of the groups. Circumstances that may make the semicolon preferable to the comma are length and complexity of the groups, the absence of a connective, or a shift of grammatical subject. And any of these same circumstances may make the period better than the semicolon. Each case must be settled by the writer according to the immediate situation. The more important a group is in its context, the more reason for preferring semicolon to comma or period to semicolon.

Compound sentences with *hence, therefore,* or *nevertheless* following a semicolon are not frequent, sentence breaks being usual before these connectives. Before *and, but, for,*

---

[8] From an editorial in *Life,* October 27, 1947. By permission.
[9] From an editorial in *The Nation,* February 21, 1948. By permission.

*or, nor*, the semicolon is less frequent than the comma. The
favorite occasion for the semicolon is a junction not marked
by a connective. Table E in the Appendix (400 two-member
compound sentences) reports 93 commas and only 22 semicolons before *and*, 66 commas and 22 semicolons before *but*,
16 commas and 2 semicolons before *for*. Of the 102 sentences
with no connectives at the junctions, the points used are
dash in 5, comma in 9, colon in 13, semicolon in 75—nearly
three fourths of the list.

2. **Marking the boundaries between expressions in series.** When
   the members are light and simple enough to be clearly grouped
   with commas, commas are usually preferable. Examples with
   semicolon:

   > Books cited in the chapter are *Webster's New International
   > Dictionary*, Second Edition; *Manuscript & Proof*, by John Ben-
   > bow; *A Manual of Style*, by the staff of the University of Chicago
   > Press, and the *Style Manual* of the Government Printing Office.
   > [Before the *and*, a comma is sufficient.]

3. Now and then **before an appositive or modifier**, with the suggestion that the second group is coordinate with the first.
   Example:

   > Of course government control will be different this time; just
   > a little control. [*Just a little control* is technically an appositive,
   > but has the feeling of a sentence member, as if it read *there will
   > be just a little control*.] . . . At the end of the war there were
   > great numbers of veterans whose lives had been shaken; men
   > qualified and willing to benefit by the training the government
   > made available to them.

The semicolon before *namely* is only a tradition. Before
*that is*, the semicolon may be useful if the following words
parallel the preceding group. For example:

> The buyer of less than a full lot or round lot, which is usually
> 100 shares, pays an "odd lot premium"; that is, he pays $12\frac{1}{2}$ cents
> more per share than the price at which his broker bought the
> shares.

**The Semicolon with Other Marks**

The semicolon may follow a closing parenthesis or bracket and either precede or follow suspension dots. It precedes or follows ellipsis dots according to the position of the omitted words, but regularly follows a closing quote. The combination of semicolon with dash is practically obsolete.

## THE DASH

When used without qualification, the name *dash* means the ordinary em dash. In addition to this, printers have the en dash—which they know and authors don't need to know—and long dashes, which are rare in text matter. The typewriter dash is commonly made by two strokes of the hyphen key without preceding or following space.

The dash has been described as the interruption, the mark of abruptness, the sob, the stammer, and the mark of ignorance. The last name—which might be equally well applied to the comma as crude writers use it—records the fact that the uninformed mistake the dash for an all-purpose mark for every possible occasion. Dashes are less frequent in good writing than commas, but usually more frequent than semicolons, parentheses, or colons. Though condemned by some as a nuisance, the dash is so useful that it has come into wide use for a variety of purposes.

The dash is an abrupt or emphatic mark, characteristically employed to mark interruption, sharp separation, or a sudden turn. It is more nearly akin to the comma than any other mark, being used alone or in pairs, between expressions either coordinate or of different rank, and in a variety of patterns. But unlike the comma it is a strong point, with a characteristic quality in spite of its versatility. The dash, either singly or in pairs, is used for the following purposes:

1. **To group words for special emphasis, or to indicate hesitation, interruption, incompletion, suspense or release of suspension, shift of structure, or emphatic repetition.** Examples:

> He began with the usual platitudes. "My young friends, I hope I can tell you something that will save you from making mistakes. When I was a boy in high school——" . . . Prices climbed—and went on climbing. . . . They will continue to rise until—well, I don't know when. . . . When a truck loaded with dynamite was hit by a passenger car ten miles east of Houston this morning, there was an explosion—a rear tire on the truck blew out. . . . After a bad morning at the office he goes out for lunch, stands in line for ten minutes before he can get a seat, gets a plate of liver and onions, which he abhors, instead of the egg salad he ordered, and—but why continue the sad story? . . . War, famine, drought, brigandage, anarchy—all these have left the country in an almost hopeless state.

2. **To mark emphatically the junction between members of compound sentences,** with the suggestion of appositive relation or of a surprising turn. For example:

> Remember to use your rear-view mirror—don't stop, slow down, or turn unless you know what's behind you. [Either colon or semicolon might replace the dash, with different effect.] . . . The postal system is deeper in the red than ever before—and some businessmen say that it's getting a bit senile.

3. **To set off parenthetical expressions, descriptive modifiers, or descriptive appositives.** For this purpose the dash competes with the lighter comma and with parentheses. Examples with dash or pair of dashes:

> His candidacy will help Republican chances—not decisively but perhaps considerably—in certain states. . . . The instruments of the concertino in Bach's Brandenburg Concerto No. 4—the solo instruments—are violin and two flutes. . . . The capacity of the proposed 27-foot channel—which will be ice-bound or fog-bound six months of every twelve—is no indication of the traffic it will carry. . . . Mr. Attlee admits that his new program will involve some sacrifice of individual liberty—by both employers and work-

ers. . . . In a pocket of a coat he had put away for the winter he found a letter he had hunted for in every imaginable place and—think of it!—a $20 bill.

4. **Between members of a series,** usually with the effect of emphasizing the following member sharply. Example:

A security market provides a place where savings can be invested for dividends and possible appreciation—and yet be available at an hour's notice if needed.

5. **To mark ellipsis of a word or part of a word** by way of concealment, delicacy, or the appearance of delicacy: "What the d——l does he mean?" This is not an important use.

6. **To serve as a ditto mark in catalog work.**

7. **Sometimes to separate a serial number from the text at the beginning of a paragraph.** But serials are more commonly punctuated with period or enclosed in parentheses.

8. **Sometimes to punctuate a run-in sidehead** that is not an integral part of the paragraph to which it belongs. More common styles are period alone or period with dash.

9. **To separate an extract from a following credit.** Example:

Persons of good sense, I have since observed, seldom fall into it [disputing about religion] except lawyers, university men, and men of all sorts that have been bred at Edinburgh.—Benjamin Franklin, *Autobiography*.

10. **Sometimes after words introducing tabular matter.** Example:

I move—

That the pending resolution be referred to the Finance Committee.

That this committee be authorized to employ an expert accountant.

The en dash or half dash, for which typewriters have no character, is used between limit year dates, sometimes in compound words that are set in capitals, and between names when one of them is written in two words. Examples: the War of 1941–45; the New York–Washington express; THE ANGLO-IRANIAN OIL PACT. Authors need not mark en dashes in copy. The printer will correct hyphens to en dashes when these are called for.

### The Dash with Other Marks

Thanks to the good work done a generation ago by printers, such ugly and unnecessary combinations as comma with dash, semicolon with dash, and colon with dash have become nearly obsolete. A dash can do all that comma with dash ever did; a colon alone is better than colon with dash after a *Dear Sir* or after words introducing a list or quotation.

A dash may follow a terminal mark (period, question mark, or exclamation) at the end of an extract when a credit to book or author follows. A run-in sidehead that does not make an integral part of its paragraph may be punctuated with period alone, with colon, with period and dash, or sometimes with dash alone. A period alone is sufficient for the purpose. Example:

> **Dash with comma, semicolon, or colon.** A safe rule is "Don't combine them."

An exclamation or question mark may be used, but is not often used, before the second of a pair of dashes enclosing a modifying, appositive, or parenthetical group. And occasionally a dash is used after the second of a pair of parentheses. With a closing quote, a dash precedes or follows according to circumstances.

## THE COLON

The colon is usually a mark of addition or expectation, with emphasis on a following explanation, list, table, or quotation. With formal words (*as follows* or the like) it raps for attention; with easy wording it is little more formal than the somewhat lighter semicolon. It is not a series or balancing point like the semicolon; it seems to say "Watch carefully what comes next." In text matter the colon has the following uses:

1. **To punctuate words that formally introduce quotations, lists, tables, or ordinary appositives.** The nearest equivalent of the colon is the less formal dash. Examples with the colon occur often in this book.

The colon is sometimes used at the end of a paragraph to mark for attention a following paragraph or passage, or replaces within a paragraph the expected period at the end of an introductory sentence. The presumption in either case is in favor of the period, with which most introductory sentences are in fact punctuated.

2. **To mark the junction between members of two-member compound sentences,** especially when no connective is used and when the second member fulfills a promise made by the first member. (This is not to say that all such sentences take the colon. For example, the favorite mark in the *It is not . . . it is* pattern is the semicolon.) Examples with colon:

   Shaw was realistic: labor must be compelled to work. . . . You know your responsibility: you have charge and are expected to get the job done.

The colon is traditionally the mark at the main junction in a compound compound sentence that uses one or more semicolons. This pattern is infrequent in American publications. Example:

   Barking dogs may not bite, but voters do; a politician up for reelection would as soon be photographed beating his wife as maltreating a dog. Presidents have been no exception: Warren G. Harding's Airedale, Laddie, Calvin Coolidge's white collie, Rob Roy, and Herbert Hoover's several hunting dogs were walking political assets; the best known of all the White House dogs was Fala, President Roosevelt's Scotty.[10] [An entire paragraph.]

Before a sentence member beginning with *but, or, nor, and,* or *for,* the colon is unusual. One expects a comma or semicolon.

3. **To group items in expressions of time and in literary references:**

> 11:30 in the morning; at 11:31:47; Otto Jespersen, *Essentials of English Grammar,* New York: Henry Holt & Co., Inc.

### The Obstructive Colon

A good many periodicals use the colon before a list in this manner:

> A rifleman who reloads center-fire ammunition needs: a decapping and recapping tool, a micrometer powder balance, and perhaps a bullet mold.

Because the colon is an unnecessary interruption between the verb and its required complement, nothing is gained by its use. After such words as *the following* there is reason for using the colon.

### The Colon with Other Marks

If introductory words calling for the colon end with a group enclosed in parentheses, the colon will immediately follow the closing parenthesis. When used with a closing quote, the colon follows the quote.

## PARENTHESES

Though the name parenthesis is often applied to an expression that might be omitted without dislocation of structure, the curved punctuation marks (   ) are usually called parentheses—"parens" among printers.

---

[10] From *Newsweek,* January 26, 1948. By permission.

In the plainest prose, parentheses are used mainly for two purposes: (1) to enclose serial numbers or letters, as in this sentence; (2) to enclose incidental explanatory matter, page references, dates, or other expressions that other points would emphasize too strongly or not distinguish clearly from the context. But parentheses may enclose whole sentences or passages, and within sentences they may set off expressions of considerable length and complexity. The other common marks of parenthetical relation are commas and dashes, both of them used oftener than parentheses.

Though parentheses seem to say "here it is if you wish it; it's only an aside," such an aside may be intended for special notice—like many a remark that begins with the disarming *by the way* or *incidentally*.

The following examples illustrate the use of parentheses to enclose incidental bits of information, parenthetical modifiers and appositives, and sentence members. For parenthetical sentences and paragraphs, see Chapters 2 and 3.

John Benbow's *Manuscript & Proof* (Oxford, 1937) has a useful chapter on the typing of manuscript. . . . The *News and Observer* (Raleigh, N.C.) was edited for many years by the late Josephus Daniels . . . The Philadelphia convention (1797) had important work to do. . . . Despite fat earnings (which are generally continuing) stocks are tending downward. . . . Grant, E. L., *Statistical Quality Control,* 1946 (311.22, G761s). . . . They complain of a dollar shortage (they should say their own shortage of funds and production). . . . See the section on communism (pages 67–88). . . . His market jargon ("double tops," "head and shoulders," "velocity ratings," "resistance points") explained nothing. . . . Sales of $820 million (including federal taxes on cigarettes) were 10 per cent up. . . . Despite his (supposedly) friendly attitude, he gave no actual help. [This illustrates an infrequent but sometimes convenient pattern.]

In citing bylaws or other rules that are marked with serials enclosed in parentheses—for example, "(A) The

President is authorized to call a special meeting at any time"—the style *Rule (A)* is often used. This is an exception to the general custom of enclosing only incidental matter within parentheses.

The use of parentheses to enclose serial numbers or letters has been mentioned. For this purpose, parentheses are specially useful within sentences or paragraphs.

Parentheses are sometimes used to enclose interpolations, especially the unflattering commentary *sic* calling attention to a slip or a peculiarity in quoted matter. If the context clearly shows that the inserted matter is an interpolation, parentheses are not seriously objectionable. Otherwise it is best to use brackets or to manage comment without interpolation. Some newspapers whose machines lack bracket characters have used parentheses regularly for interpolations in quoted matter.

Parentheses are infrequently used within words to enclose doubtful or alternative letters, as when one writes *the strai(gh)t and narrow way, the owner(s),* by way of pointing out the proper spelling *strait* and uncertainty whether *owner* should take singular or plural form.

## Parentheses with Other Marks

The closing parenthesis follows a sentence point only when the whole sentence or passage is parenthetical. If parentheses enclose a group at the end (for example, *page 232* or *see Chart A*), the parenthesis stands inside the period or other sentence point. A comma, semicolon, colon, or dash may immediately follow a closing parenthesis. A closing quote precedes or follows a closing parenthesis according to the material of the quotation.

A question mark or exclamation marking the character of parenthetical material stands inside the closing parenthesis, thus:

His "efficient and effective" plan (how he loves those adjectives!) was not adopted. . . . This "undemocratic" zoning ordinance (is it actually undemocratic?) has a good chance of being enacted.

## SUSPENSION DOTS

Suspension dots or "French dots" (*points de suspension*) occur in groups, usually of three, usually spaced but sometimes closed up. They mark preceding matter as unfinished, or left dangling an instant for attention. They are used within sentences or as terminal points—sometimes in place of the usual sentence point, sometimes in addition. (Ellipsis dots, in the same form, are discussed in Chapter 9.)

Suspension dots sometimes occur in articles in the better magazines, but belong specially to fiction and advertising. (In the 2,000 sentences represented by Table A in the Appendix there are no suspension dots.)

The use of suspension dots was long ago satirized by Don Marquis in the New York *Evening Sun:*

> Whenever you see . . . three little dots . . . such as these . . . in the stuff of a modern versifier . . . even in our stuff . . . it means that the writer . . . is trying to suggest something rather . . . well, elusive, if you get what we mean . . . and the reason he suggests it instead of expressing it . . . is . . . very often . . . because it is an almost idea . . . instead of a real idea . . .

*Newsweek* and certain other periodicals have found a good use for the "three little dots"—to mark boundaries between discontinuous material within what looks like a single paragraph. For example, *Newsweek* saves four paragraph breaks in the material under the heading Trends Abroad (February 2, 1948) by using suspension dots (without additional sentence points) as marks of division.

## BRACKETS

Brackets have only one common use—to enclose material interpolated within quoted matter by way of explanation, comment, or substitution. (See Chapter 9.) The use of brackets within parentheses to mark secondary parenthesis is rare, commas or dashes being usual. Because the standard typewriter keyboard has no bracket characters, one who needs brackets must insert them by hand.

Certain dictionaries bracket information about derivation of words, and writers who use phonetic symbols in spelling text bracket the symbols or transcribed words: *Beetle* has six letters but only four sounds [bitl]; *school, tax,* and *quit* have [k] but not *k*; *debt* and *doubt* have *b* but not [b].

# CHAPTER 9

## QUOTATIONS

Quotation points include not only the familiar double and single quotation marks (herein called by the printer's name quotes) but also marks of omission or interpolation and structural marks used where quotations are introduced, interrupted, or resumed.

The printer's double quotes are usually in the shape of two inverted commas (opening) and two apostrophes (closing), single quotes being a single inverted comma and a single apostrophe. Standard typewriter quotes are the same in form for both beginning and end. Save for quotation within quotation, most American printers use double quotes for both citation and special designation. But there are exceptions. The Oxford University Press, for example, uses single quotes for both citation and special designation, reserving double quotes for secondary quotations. Certain other publications differentiate by using double quotes for ordinary citation (with single quotes for secondary quotations) and single quotes for words named as words or terms with special meaning. The distinction between citation and special designation is sometimes convenient.

Quote marks are used to indicate direct borrowing of phraseology or to mark expressions as special, peculiar, or of such flavor that the writer wishes to rid himself of responsibility. Indirect quotation is no occasion for the use of quotes; but as a matter of course one may embed a direct quotation in words cited in substance:

> He told his students that he expected them to do in language study just what a biologist does in the study of biology—"to observe, to classify, and to make true generalizations."

Anyone who quotes another person's words has the duty of keeping the words unchanged and continuous or of giving clear notice to the contrary. It is improper to alter wording or punctuation of quoted matter, to italicize words without due notice, or to make any other change that would misrepresent the meaning of the quoted words in their context. And of course every omission or insertion should be duly marked unless the quotation is confessedly a mosaic.

## Quotes and White Space

Quote marks sprinkled all over a page are not beautiful. The scholarly printer Theodore Low De Vinne considered it unfortunate that when the English printers decided to mark quotations they refused the French form—a reversible mark that occupies the middle of the face. Concerning the marks the English printers adopted (a pair of reversed commas for beginning and a pair of apostrophes for closing quote), De Vinne says, "The apostrophe on the five-to-em body is made thinner than the comma on the four-to-em body, and their knobby endings are not in true line. Unlike other characters in the font, they occupy the upper part of the body, and leave an unsightly blank below, often to the detriment of even spacing." Though some modern fonts include a special beginning quote, the white gaps remain.

## A Note on the Rhetoric of Quotation

Quotation is attended with certain dangers—of unduly emphasizing the form of the quoted words when indirect quotation would be better, or of making a patchwork of matter that should be original. Whatever the writer's intention, quotes emphasize whatever they enclose. Because the marks with their white gaps catch the eye, they effect a sort of grouping that resembles structural punctuation. Quotes are particularly bad when they call attention to the writer's supposedly clever wording or when they turn an ordinary name into a nickname. Examples:

> His "discourteous courtesy," as I once called it, made him ridiculous. . . . I always keep an "eagle eye" on the Dow-Jones averages. . . . Mrs. Stowe wrote her famous book while "keeping house" in Brunswick. . . . A country dentist's name plate: John Doe, "Dentist."

## Omitting Quote Marks

Quotes may be advantageously omitted under the following circumstances:

1. When the expression is common property: new wine in old bottles; a millstone about his neck; a house divided against itself; it smells to heaven; waifs and strays; a pig in a poke; enough and to spare.

2. When the context gives adequate credit. But an indirect quotation may be supplemented with a direct quotation. For example:

> In his famous remark concerning the perfect sentence ("the sentence so fortunately born, 'entire, smooth, and round,' that it needs no punctuation") Walter Pater used fifteen marks in a single sentence—eleven commas, a pair of parentheses, a colon reinforced with dash, and a terminal exclamation mark.

3. When the quotation is a quotation only in form: As the Governor of North Carolina said to the Governor of South Carolina, it's a long time between drinks. When this twentieth century Romeo first saw his Juliet, he said to himself, This is it!

4. When the boundaries of the quotation are made clear by change of type face, shortening of lines, or other mechanical means. A run-in quotation (one that does not begin a new paragraph) need not be in quotes if set in italic or boldface. Nor is there need to use quotes for reduced-type extracts set as separate paragraphs, unless they are in series without clear indication of their origin and discontinuity.

There is no general agreement regarding choice between the run-in style with quotes and the reduced-type style, except that short quotations and quotations of less than a sentence, however long, are commonly run in. But exceptions are made for the sake of emphasis or uniformity.

In some publications reduced-type extracts or extracts set in shorter measure of the same type face are regularly enclosed in quotes. Each office has its rules.

In double-spaced typewritten matter, extracts are often written in shorter lines with single spacing.

In reports of debates and proceedings, the occurrence of the speaker's name or of Q. and A. (for Question and Answer) before each part of the dialog makes quotes unnecessary.

> The PRESIDING OFFICER. Shall the bill pass?
>
> Mr. SMITH. I ask for the yeas and nays.

## Quote Marks for Special Designation

Quotes are often used to mark nicknames, misnomers, slang phrases, technical or unusual phrases; translations or paraphrases; names of ships; titles of books, periodicals, poems, and works of musical or plastic art; and expressions used with satirical intent, the quotes meaning "so called."

A rule that quotes must be used in all these cases or in any one of them would be misleading. First, an expression once marked as slang, once defined, or once marked as a nickname may thereafter be treated as an ordinary word. Again, there is some latitude of choice—not in any one office—between quotes and italic. For example, names of ships are italicized by some publishers, quoted by others, and sometimes set in roman type without quotes. Foreign phrases that have not become familiar are usually italicized; but foreign extracts exceeding a few words in length may be treated as if they were English.

When book titles appear in italic, as they usually do in

text matter, it is convenient to enclose chapter titles in quotes. Quotes are also suitable for titles of lectures, short poems, and magazine articles. Rules of style vary from office to office.

Some titles require neither quotes nor italic, whatever style is used for other titles. It is not necessary to quote or italicize the names Bible or New Testament, The Gettysburg Address, The Iliad, Introduction, Preface, or chapter titles in a series of more than three or four.

One may save bad effects by composing with an eye to the publisher's styles. The following are clumsy because italic in one example and quotes in the other are used for two purposes:

> The expressions *our mutual friend* and the *two first* are mentioned in *The Standard of Usage in English Speech.* . . . For the terms "suppression of clauses" and "weight of prediction," see L. A. Sherman's "Analytics of Literature."

Whether to include *the, an,* or *a* in a quoted or italicized title is a matter of judgment. Books with such titles as *A History of American Literature* and *The Social Contract* may be named in either quote or italic style with or without the articles. Examples without *a* or *the,* which would seem stiff:

> For an account of the Knickerbocker writers, see Cairns's *History of American Literature.* . . . Rousseau's *Social Contract* was widely read in western Europe.

When book titles are written roman open, an initial *the, an,* or *a* is capitalized if exact citation is desirable, but otherwise need not be. When titles of periodicals are italicized or enclosed in quotes, *the* is commonly left outside the boundaries of the italic or quotes. If the roman open style is used, the article need not take a capital. Examples:

> **Quote style:** an article in the "Atlantic Monthly."
> **Italic style:** an article in the *Atlantic Monthly.*
> **Roman open style:** an editorial in the Dallas Morning News.

Certain periodicals regularly keep the article *the* in referring to themselves: *The Saturday Evening Post, The Nation.*

## Words Named as Words

When words are named as words, the usual options are quote marks (double or single according to the publisher's style) and italic. But sometimes the context makes such indication unnecessary, as in the third example below.

> **Double quotes:** The word "doctrine" has a religious association.
>
> **Italic:** *Stirrup* is an amalgamated compound.
>
> **Roman open:** The term profit has a special meaning in economics.

## Secondary Quotations

When double quotes mark primary run-in quotations, as in most American offices, a secondary quotation (quotation within quotation) is enclosed in single quotes. If single quotes enclose primary quotations, as in books of the Oxford University Press, secondary quotations take double quotes. Examples:

> As Hazlitt remarks, "The 'housing shortage' is itself in large part a product of the very rent control that 'protects' us from it."
>
> John Benbow says, 'Authors are likely to assume that a professional typist will observe consistency, and they take it for granted also that "the printer looks out for all that." As a matter of fact, in these days of machine composition, the printer does not "look out for all that," and the changing of the author's spelling, capitalization, and punctuation cannot safely be left to the printer's discretion.' [1] [Single quotes for primary, double for secondary, according to the style of the Oxford University Press.]

If a secondary quotation occurs within a reduced-type extract not enclosed in quotes, primary quote marks are used.

[1] *Manuscript & Proof.* Copyright 1937, the Oxford University Press, New York. By permission.

A tertiary quotation, if the writer is daring enough to use such a thing and if he can count on his reader to thread the maze, will be enclosed in the marks used for primary quotations. Good advice: Don't use a quotation within a quotation within a quotation.

### Repeating Quote Marks

In a continuous extract of two or more paragraphs with which quotes are used, it is customary to use the opening quote at the beginning of each paragraph and the closing quote only at the end of the last. The old fashion of using an opening quote at the beginning of each line of a run-in extract is obsolete.

### Structural Points Before Quotations

A dependent quotation may be preceded by any one of several marks, or may be treated as an open sentence element. The popular notion that a quoted group must be preceded by a comma or colon is an error that induces waste of good punctuation marks. Examples with and without preceding punctuation:

He quoted Pascal's saying that "reason makes her friends only miserable." [Integral sentence element.]

The Preamble begins with the words "We, the people of the United States." [Defining appositive.]

He called out "Get going, boys."

The chairman asked him, "Have I stated your motion correctly?"

The last German Kaiser said at Bremen, "We, the Hohenzollern, regard ourselves as appointed by God to govern and lead the people whom it is given us to rule." [A very frequent style, with comma.]

Article X of the Bill of Rights (Rights of States under Constitution) reads as follows: "The powers not delegated to the United

States by the Constitution, nor prohibited by it to the States, are reserved to the States respectively, or to the people." [*As follows* calls for the colon.]

The Kaiser's doctrine of divine right—"We, the Hohenzollern, regard ourselves as appointed by God to govern and lead the people whom it is given us to rule"—was an anachronism. [Quotation in apposition.]

They went swimming in the Great Salt Lake ("you float in that water"). [Parenthetical quotation.]

Hazlitt ridicules the idea. "What the world is suffering from today is not a dollar crisis. It is a sterling crisis, a franc crisis, a guilder crisis, a peso crisis. It staggers from crisis to crisis because it will not allow free markets to function." [2] [Quotation begins after a sentence break; a useful pattern.]

"Shakespeare never repeats." Nonsense. Have you counted how many times we are told in *Othello* that Iago is known to be honest? [Quotation a separate sentence, comment following.]

### Interruption and Resumption of Quotations

When a quotation is interrupted by such an expression as *he said* or *he continued* or *says Mr. Roberts*, it is usual to have a comma within the closing quote and another after the interrupter:

"The back of inflation," said Mr. Zelomek, "has been broken."

. . . "An experienced writer," says Arlo Bates, "means a point as definitely as he means a word." [Point means punctuation mark.]

If a quotation is followed by a tag, the pattern is as follows:

"Lower prices at the grocery counter may be expected within six weeks," he said.

The less frequent patterns—either no point or a dash at the place where the quotation is broken—may be illustrated by the following examples:

---

[2] Henry Hazlitt in *Newsweek*, August 18, 1947. By permission.

"Nobody believes the newspapers" a cynic once remarked. . . .
"Oh—" she murmured, being for once in her life unable to say anything.

As a matter of course an interrupted quotation may be resumed after a semicolon or at a period within or at the end of a paragraph.

"You are right," said Mr. Allen; "our government knows all the answers and will make all the decisions."

The important report published under the title *American English Grammar* has much to say against present methods of teaching English grammar and usage. "It is the point of view of this report *that a study of the real grammar of Present-day English has never been used in the schools* and that the conclusions concerning its effectiveness relate only to the type of 'grammar' that has been tried. The 'grammar' hitherto used in the schools has been either the logical analysis of sentences and 'parsing,' most often illustrated by the various methods of diagramming, or a learning of rules and definitions which were assumed to be the measures of correct language."

Fries continues in the next paragraph: "In the light of the principles which underlie our investigation this customary use of 'grammar' is fundamentally unsound. First, language usage cannot thus be separated into two simple classes [*correct forms and mistakes*]. Instead, our usage presents a complex range of differing and changing practices which must be understood in relation to the feelings of an indefinite number of social groups. Second, sensitiveness to usage—a richness of assimilated experience through which one becomes aware of the suggestions attaching to words and constructions because of the circumstances in which they are commonly used—is the only condition upon which good English can be won. All the effort which goes to make one *conscious* of 'rules of grammar' serves to deaden this sensitiveness to one's speech environment and to turn one's attention away from the only source of real knowledge." [3] [Italic in the original. The second part of the citation is a complete paragraph.]

[3] From Charles Carpenter Fries, *American English Grammar*, p. 285 f. D. Appleton-Century Co., New York. By permission.

### Order of Quotes and Structural Marks

When a closing quote and a structural mark occur together, the usual American rules of order are as follows:

1. Both comma and period stand inside the closing quote. (A comma or period preceding a beginning quote is separated from it by space.)

    "This," he said, "is our standing rule."

2. The question or exclamation mark stands inside the closing quote if it is intended to give interrogative or exclamatory character to the quoted group.

    "Is that your intention?" the chairman inquired. . . . The chairman inquired, "Is that your intention?" . . . "Watch that car!" she exclaimed. . . . She exclaimed, "Watch that car!"

    If an interrogative or exclamatory sentence happens to end with a quoted expression, the question or exclamation point that marks the sentence as a whole will follow the quote.

    Did the report of the committee use the ugly words "grossly incompetent management"? . . . He has unblushingly described himself as "an acknowledged authority"!

3. A semicolon or colon is placed outside the closing quote.

    They complain of a "dollar crisis," "a shortage of dollars"; they should say a shortage of pesos, guilders, francs, or pounds. . . . Prediction concerning this impending "major depression": it won't come this year.

4. Marks of omission, usually ellipsis dots but sometimes asterisks, precede the closing quote. Otherwise they fail to show that words have been omitted. Of course the absence of ellipsis pointing does not imply that the extract is complete, such pointing being required only when there is need to call attention to an omission. If a rule of the University of Chicago Press were cited in abbreviated form, it would appear as follows: "Where references to the same work follow each other closely and uninterruptedly, use *ibid.* instead of repeating the title. . . ."

5. An interruption dash belonging to a quotation precedes the closing quote. A dash marking the end of an appositive quoted phrase, or belonging in any other way to the original rather than the quoted part, follows the closing quote.

> "If only I could write—" he sadly remarked. . . . His easy rule—"buy when they are low, sell when they are high"—is hard to apply. When are they low? When are they high?

6. Suspension dots (structural marks, not marks of ellipsis) will serve their purpose at the end of a quotation only if they are put outside the closing quote.

> He sadly remarked, "If I only had a good vocabulary" . . .

7. Quote marks belonging to a parenthetical quotation within dashes or parentheses stand within the marks of parenthesis.

> David Ross Locke ("Petroleum V. Nasby") was a popular American humorist. . . . My teacher learned his favorite slogan— "use the right word and not its second cousin"—from Mark Twain.

8. The apostrophe stands inside the quote mark.

> The song "Feudin' and Fightin'" was then familiar.

### Double and Single Quotes Together

With period or comma, the usual order is period or comma, secondary quote, primary quote. In ordinary American practice this means period or comma, single quote, double quote.

> "Another kind of semantic change," Roberts continued, "is called by the unfamiliar name 'pejoration.'" He explained as follows: "Some words have taken on less favorable meanings. For example, *villain* originally meant a farm laborer; it has come to mean a scoundrel." . . . "This sharp decline, hopefully described as a 'normal correction,'" he said, "may mark a major turning point."

With question or exclamation mark, the order is according to circumstances.

"What do *you* think of 'Sweeney Among the Nightingales'?"
he asked me. . . . "After long debate that got nowhere, an impatient member broke the spell by shouting 'Question, Mr. Chairman! Question!' "

## Capital or Lowercase at Beginning of Quotation

There is an obstinate popular notion that quotations, except only short phrases, must begin with capitals. There are important exceptions:

1. When quotations are in series.

   Though his wisdom had gone stale, Polonius gave his son some useful maxims: "give every man thy ear, but few thy voice"; "neither a borrower nor a lender be"; "to thine own self be true."

2. When the quotation is an ordinary sentence element.

   It has been said that "every Englishman is an island." . . . As the grammarian John Earle correctly says, "punctuation is a good servant but a bad master."

After such introductions as *He added, He began as follows, He continued,* a quotation in sentence or paragraph form will ordinarily begin with a capital. Even if a quotation is a defining appositive or the complement of a verb, sentence form usually calls for an initial capital.

The question "Which pronunciation is correct?" is often answered positively upon scanty information. . . . It is easy to ask "Which pronunciation is correct?" The answer is not always easy. There are variant standard pronunciations of many a word—*soot,* for example, or *roof,* or *research.*

## Quotations Edited by Insertion or Omission

Words interpolated in quoted matter by way of explanation, comment, correction, or substitution are customarily enclosed within brackets. Newspapers whose machines lack bracket characters use parentheses for this purpose, and it is not uncommon to enclose the commentary *sic* in parentheses even when bracket characters are available. But brackets are safer because their intent is unmistakable. Even the interpolation of a question or exclamation mark by way of comment ought to be marked as an interpolation. If editing takes the form of italicizing for emphasis, the fact should be made clear—"Italic not in the original" or the like.

For omission of words from quoted matter, the customary sign is a group of spaced periods (ellipses), less often asterisks, in addition to any structural mark required at the spot where the omission begins. The number of periods or asterisks is usually three, but not always. (The University of Chicago Press uses four dots separated by three-to-em spaces, in addition to the sentence period if the omission comes at the end of a declarative sentence.)

The following example illustrates the use of both brackets and ellipses:

> Beveridge quoted the glowing prophecy of a Boston journal:
>
> "Liberty will have another feather in her cap. . . . The ensuing winter [1789] will be the commencement of a Golden Age."

Ellipsis marks are treated as part of the quotation and accordingly are within the quotes. *Etc.* may be within the quotes or not according to circumstances—within the quotes when the reader would otherwise not understand that *etc.* stands for an omitted part of the quoted matter.

For ellipsis of a paragraph or more, it is customary to use a full line of spaced periods, less often a line of spaced asterisks. Rules vary from office to office.

Insertion and omission need to be managed with care. If bracketed groups or ellipses are badly placed, the effect can be awkward.

> Ugly thoughts and painful doubts will arise; and the earth . . . to the mature man or woman seldom remains a place of simple joy and gladness, but the home rather of . . . misery.

There was lacking in [Rousseau] the control of a well balanced intellect, which might have controlled his capricious and extravagant emotions.

When part of a sentence has been omitted, the remainder may be united into one sentence with following matter—not necessarily the next sentence, ellipsis marks being indefinite as to the extent of the omission. As a matter of course the borrower has the responsibility of seeing that the abbreviated quotation represents the meaning accurately.

# CHAPTER 10

## COMPOUND WORDS AND OPEN COMPOUNDS

(The following abbreviations are used in this chapter: **ACD,** *American College Dictionary*; **GPO,** *Style Manual* of the United States Government Printing Office; **UCP,** *A Manual of Style* of the University of Chicago Press; **WNID,** *Webster's New International Dictionary*, Second Edition.)

According to the usual definition, a compound word is a solid or hyphened unit made up of two or more words that have independent status, such as the parts of *handbook* or *self-evident*. Though words made of combining forms or of a word with one or more affixes are sometimes called compounds, they are more strictly called derivatives. Specimen derivatives are *thermograph,* the parts of which are Greek combining forms, and *unlikelihood,* with the stem *like* and the affixes *un, li, hood.* This distinction between compounds and derivatives will be observed in this chapter.

Compound words include nouns (*textbook, self-reliance*), adjectives (*waterproof, saber-toothed*), verbs (*broadcast, dry-clean*), prepositions (*upon, throughout*), conjunctions (*whereas, inasmuch as*), adverbs (*somewhat, well-nigh*), and pronouns (*himself, something, whatever*). Because the real difficulties in compounding are experienced with the forms of nouns and adjectives, little need be said about other compounds.

Though French and Latin influence after the Norman Conquest took from English much of its former facility and activity in compounding, the creation of compounds now goes on apace, to the great benefit of the language. For example, the English vocabulary has been greatly enriched by the creation of the verb *air-condition* and the nouns *newsprint, acre-foot, kilowatt-hour, airman, airfield, blueprint,* and *skyscraper,* each of which says clearly what might otherwise require half a dozen words.

### Three Kinds of Compounds

It is impossible to understand compounds without recognizing a kind that is not included in the usual definition. In addition to solid and hyphened compound words, all of us use freely a third and very important kind of compound exemplified by *post office, gas engine, fishing rod.* These need not be called compound words, because "word" is usually understood to mean a unit separated from its neighbors by spacing. For this reason such forms as *gas engine* and *fishing rod* will be called open compounds in this chapter. (In speech, the real language, they are clearly compounds.)

The following entries in *Webster's Collegiate Dictionary,* Fifth Edition, illustrate the three types.[1] The definitions show that each is a unit expression with a specialized meaning.

> gold'fish' (-fish'), *n.; pl.,* see FISH. **1.** A small cyprinoid fish (*Carassius auratus*), chiefly golden-yellow or orange, kept in aquariums and ponds. **2.** *Army Slang.* Salmon.

> gold'-filled' (gōld'fĭld'; 2), *adj. Jewelry.* Covered with a layer of gold so as to constitute filled gold.

> gold point. *Finance.* In foreign exchange, the rate of exchange at which it is as cheap to settle accounts by the shipment of gold as it is to do so by buying exchange.

Both meanings and accents show that such names as *gold point* and *post office* are not phrases but true compounds. As John S. Kenyon says in his valuable Guide to Pronuncia-

---

[1] Copyright 1936, 1941, by G. & C. Merriam Co., Springfield, Mass. By permission.

tion (WNID, p. xxxv), "it must be remembered that pronunciation (esp. accent) and meaning constitute word compounds, not the manner of writing them." To use Kenyon's illustration, *cooking apples* is a compound when it means apples *for* cooking, not a compound when it means apples that *are* cooking. The two meanings are marked by different stress patterns.

## Specialized Meaning and Classifying Stress

The marks of the typical compound noun are specific meaning, either literal or figurative, and classifying stress. In the following two-member compound nouns the members that carry primary stress are set in CAPITALS, members carrying secondary stress are in SMALL CAPITALS: BLACKJACK, REDFISH, MOSSBACK, BLACKSMITH, EGGPLANT, GRAPEFRUIT, TEXTBOOK, FOOTBALL. Though some compounds have lost the usual secondary stress (*postman, sixpence, breakfast*), the usual stress pattern in two-member compound nouns is the one just illustrated—primary stress on the first member, secondary stress on the second member. This stress pattern marks, for example, the fact that BLACKJACK has a special figurative meaning (bludgeon or pirate flag, according to the context), that REDFISH is a specific kind of fish and not merely a fish with red coloring, and so on for the other specimens. The *Webster's Collegiate Dictionary* entry *goldfish* marks the primary and secondary accents. In the entry *gold point* no accents are shown; the stress pattern is GOLD POINT.[2]

---

[2] For authoritative information about accents in compounds, see (1) WNID, Guide to Pronunciation, secs. 60–67 (pp. xxxiv–xxxvi) and (2) John S. Kenyon and Thomas A. Knott, *A Pronouncing Dictionary of American English,* Introduction, secs. 48–53. This dictionary lists numerous compounds such as *cold-blooded, college-bred, drugstore, drumhead, dry-clean,* and marks the accents. In entries for compound adjectives the dictionary repeatedly illustrates the fact that an attributive compound adjective (preceding its noun) normally gives the first member primary stress, as in *college-bred man.*

In many compounds the words change from their usual grammatical functions. For example, the verb *knock* and the adverb *out* become a compound noun in *third-round knock-out,* with primary accent on *knock*; and an adjective-noun phrase *third round* has been made into a compound adjective THIRD-ROUND. In SKINFLINT the verb *skin* and its object noun *flint* have been fused into a compound noun.

### Specializing vs. Descriptive Stress

In the obvious remark that a crow is a *black bird* but not a *blackbird,* the adjective-noun phrase *black bird* has descriptive stress, marking the meaning "bird with black plumage"; the compound BLACKBIRD is specific. The following examples illustrate the radical difference between compounds and phrases:

| COMPOUNDS WITH DEFINING STRESS | PHRASES WITH DESCRIPTIVE STRESS |
| --- | --- |
| The *boiling point* at sea level | Cooked in *boiling water* |
| *Standing room* only | A *standing offer* |
| *Swimming pools* | *Swimming goslings* |
| The deadly *coral snake* | A beautiful *coral necklace* |
| A low *melting point* | *Melting snow* |
| Is it *closing time*? | In the *closing hours* |

### Anomalies in Compounding

Practice in the choice of solid, hyphened, and open forms is a queer mixture. It is based partly on the year-to-year and day-to-day decisions of copy editors and proofreaders, who are necessarily guided by what they find in dictionaries and stylebooks, partly on the intelligent or mistaken personal choices of editors and writers, partly on fine-spun theories of what ought to be. Upon a superficial view, one is tempted to say that the name of our system of compounding is Chaos, and that this chaos is a disgrace to American typography and American lexicography. Certain it is that stylebooks do not always agree with each other or with the dictionaries, or the dictionaries with each other. For example, one finds *stepping stone* in the ACD, *steppingstone* in WNID and the *New College Standard Dictionary*. Two of these dictionaries have *waiting room*; the other makes it *waiting-room*. And in three admirable books by professional printers one finds *foot-note* and *footnote, proof-reader* and *proofreader, galley-proofs* and *galley proofs, title-page* and *title page*. It is not surprising to find John Benbow saying that consistent use of the hyphen is impossible and that "if you take hyphens seriously you will surely go mad."

But an examination and comparison of the entries in the better dictionaries will make it clear that the dictionary makers are careful and well informed and that they have done their best to attain as high a degree of consistency as the stubborn facts of usage and the strange ways of our written language allow them to attain. If many of their decisions are arbitrary, these have to be arbitrary, as any proofreader knows by daily experience. And of course the dictionary makers are largely bound by the past. As they well know, the logic of any theory that calls for wholesale changes of forms according to patterns will run headlong into the inexorable logic of facts. For example, a theory that all specific noun-noun compound nouns made of short members and marked by defining stress must be closed up in German fashion has no chance of being accepted by printers or by the public. For one thing, it is an accepted general principle that solid or hyphened compounds should be made only when the one-word form is required for clearness. And though patterns have much to do with forms, there are different forms for certain patterns. Nothing short of an American academy with powers equal to those of the French Academy could reduce the forms of compounds to law and order.[3]

---

[3] F. Horace Teall's *Compounding of English Words* (1891) was an able "first systematic attempt to disentangle the perplexities of English compounding." Teall's list of inseparable (solid) compounds was ahead of his

## Considerations in the Choice of Forms

The basic rule is "no unnecessary visible compounding"—no solid or hyphened compound if the open words give the same meaning. The other considerations are clearness, consistency, and agreement with familiar custom. From the reader's point of view, clearness comes first. If an open form requires the reader to regroup words that should be hyphened or closed up, the bad form checks the reader's progress. For example, *look out* used as a noun must be solidified into *lookout; warm blooded* used as a unit modifier of *animals* should read *warm-blooded*. If a hyphen splits a natural unit or suggests an absurd meaning or a queer pronunciation (*look-out, unco-ordinated, unself-conscious*), hyphenation is bad. If forms within a single work or within the staff departments of a periodical are noticeably inconsistent, typography is to that extent bad. So far as forms violate established custom, they get unfavorable attention.

Though there is no American authority that can legislate for all cases, certain customs are well agreed upon, and there are stylebooks for individual offices. For example, government printing follows GPO styles. The GPO *Style Manual* provides for acceptable and consistent forms by some three pages of general rules and a 31-page Guide to Compounding in fine print, two columns to the page. For *hand* alone there are 124 entries, specifying *handbag, handballer, hand-bank* (verb), and so on to *hand-written, hand-wrought*.

---

day and is still useful. His system was applied by the Funk and Wagnalls *Standard Dictionary* (1893) and its successors. Alice Morton Ball's *Compounding in the English Language* (1939, reprinted with corrections 1941) is a systematic attempt to set up a rational system of compounding. When Ball specifies solid forms, she appears to be always right; but the irresistible trend of the time is against some of her hyphenations—*training-school, coloring-matter, walking-stick,* and (as nouns) *cut-off, break-down.* Ball supervised the forms of compounds in the *New College Standard Dictionary* (1947). The most useful book on compounding is Edward N. Teall's *Meet Mr. Hyphen* (1937). Unlike Ball, Teall recognized open compounds and correctly predicted increasing use of them.

The following pages outline the more important customs and considerations. It is to be noted that one consideration may conflict with another and that compounds of similar length and pattern do not necessarily take similar forms. For example, one finds solid *skyscraper* and open *shoe scraper* (both GPO forms). The figurative meaning of *skyscraper* is good reason for the solid form of this fine American word.

## COMPOUND NOUNS

In the WNID article *compound* (3b)—a mine of information about forms and patterns of compound words and other compounds—two remarks are specially important: (1) that compound nouns are "usually solid (*blackboard*) or separate (*post office*)" and (2) that compound nouns have often become solid "when the meaning is specialized or figurative and when the accent is partly or altogether lost on the second element, esp. when the first element is of one or two syllables."

"When the accent is partly lost" presumably refers to secondary accent, because the three specimens given are *blackbird, blockhead,* and *addlehead,* each of which has a secondary accent on the second member. Examples of compounds with unstressed second members are *journeyman* and *vineyard.* It is clear that in making its decisions the WNID staff considered accent, length of members, and meaning of the compound, as one would have expected.

A third remark in the same article gives an important clue to the anomalies that stare one in the face in any dictionary or stylebook: "Certain words, mostly of one syllable . . . nearly always [as second members] form solid compounds if the meaning is specific and the first element has one or two syllables." The twenty-five words listed are *ache, bane, berry, bird, board, book, boy, bush, craft, fish, flower, foot, head, hound, house, man, mouth, room, shop, weed, woman, wood, work, wort, yard.*

Application of this WNID list or of similar and perhaps longer lists by dictionary staffs or makers of stylebooks may well account for the curious fact that solid form is given to numerous compounds at the same time that many specific compounds of equal length and similar stress pattern take open form. For example, GPO specifies *brakehead, brake drum, brake shoe; cowyard, cow shed; braincap, brain pan; hand saw, handrail; ash bin, ashcan, ashpit, ashtray.* UCP has *textbook, check book; bookstore, drug store; band saw, bandstand; bucket-shop, policy shop.* The ACD has solid *bombsight,* open *bomb rack; woodlark, wood grouse; corn meal, oatmeal.*

To mourn over such anomalies would be a waste of time. Printers and dictionary makers must make decisions. If some of these decisions seem arbitrary, there is usually a good reason behind them—a desire, for example, to provide for shifting accent (CORN MEAL or CORN MEAL) by using the open form *corn meal.* When they give open form to a compound that might be solid, they know that the public is so accustomed to open compounds that one gets the meaning promptly from such forms as *slide rule, check list, dry goods, coral snake, cross section, cold front, post office,* and *money order.*

### Solid Compound Nouns

Considerations that favor solid form, without always requiring it, are brevity of the members, familiar use of the resulting compound, and specific meaning of the compound, especially figurative or technical meaning. Except in weakened compounds such as *handkerchief,* the unity of the solid compound noun is marked by the primary-secondary stress pattern. The following specimens illustrate some of the common patterns:

**Noun and noun:** newsprint, baseball and football, thumbtack, grapefruit, earthquake, rattlesnake, archerfish, battleship, satinwood, watercourse, candlepower.

**Adjective and noun:** blueprint, bluefish, deadline, hothouse, rawhide, quicksand, blackberry, yellowhammer, hummingbird, mockingbird.

**Verb and adverb:** knockout, walkover, showdown, breakdown, cutoff, cutout, pickup (of a phonograph), turnover, holdover, lockout, workout, washout. (A rule sometimes enforced is to hyphen if silent e precedes a vowel letter that begins the adverbial member: tie-up, flare-up, make-up. And nonce compounds in this pattern, or compounds that keep a nonce flavor, are hyphened: go-between, mock-up, stand-in, follow-up.)

**Adverb and verb:** downfall, downpour, bypass, offshoot, outlook, output, outcast, upshot, upstart, upkeep.

**Verb and object noun:** breakwater, scapegoat, skinflint, scarecrow, telltale, pickpocket, cutthroat, stopgap, dreadnaught. (But WNID and ACD specify kill-joy.)

**Object noun followed by actor or action noun:** taxpayer, housekeeper, storekeeper, strikebreaker, strikebreaking, sightseer, yardmaster, ringleader, policyholder, typesetter, manslaughter, proofreader, caretaker. (Certain compounds in this pattern take open form: copy editor, tank destroyer, cash register, window dresser, factory owner, range finder, aircraft carrier. Hyphened forms in this pattern, unfortunately common, are becoming archaic.)

**Preposition and noun:** downstairs (also used as adjective or adverb), overhead.

### Hyphened Compound Nouns

In general, hyphened forms are good when general usage has agreed on them, or when a new name is improvised for an immediate purpose, or when the compound keeps the flavor of a nonce compound even after long use. An unnecessary hyphen splits a natural unit or unnecessarily unites to the eye a compound that is familiar and clear in open form. The hyphened form *show-down* (instead of the usual *showdown*) calls unnecessary attention to the structure of a good American word. If *standing room* takes the form *standing-room*, the hyphen makes a half-coalesced word out of a clear and familiar open form. Examples of hyphened compound nouns:

**Nonce compounds:** first-nighting at theaters, a pick-me-up before dinner, also-rans, has-beens, so-and-sos.

**Compound numerals:** twenty-one, ninety-nine. (Spelled-out fractional nouns need no hyphens: two thirds of the membership, a half dollar.)

**Certain words of family relationship:** son-in-law, great-grandfather, great-great-grandson. (But solid granddaughter, grandfather.)

**Compounds with coordinate members:** carpenter-contractor, actor-manager, secretary-treasurer, broker-dealer, radio-phonograph, acre-foot, kilowatt-hour, city-state. (The last might take open form as an appositional phrase—"a city that is also a state.")

**Self compounds:** self-deception, self-reliance.

**Compounds of three or more members:** good-for-nothings, free-for-alls, four-in-hands, will-o'-the-wisp, jack-in-the-pulpit.

**Compounds beginning with genitives carrying apostrophe:** bird's-eye, bull's-eye, cat's-paw (figurative meaning), crow's-nest (lookout station). But solid forms hogshead, sheepshead (fish), cockscomb, hartshorn, swansdown, bridesmaid, beeswax, doomsday, ratsbane. Standard plant names in this pattern used by the Department of Agriculture (GPO, 179ff.) carry some hyphens for the sake of clearness but do not carry apostrophes: birdsnest, birdseye, cats-ear, bishopscap, Venusbutton. Standard open forms (recorded by WNID): stone's throw, stone's cast. Another dictionary uses apostrophe and hyphen in these.

**Noun with *er* and adverb:** runner-up, whipper-in, breaker-off, a snapper-up of unconsidered trifles, higher-ups, lookers-on (but onlookers).

**Compounds or phrases with elect and ex:** president-elect, ex-governor (GPO style). Competing but less frequent style: president elect, ex governor.

**Capital letter or letters with following numeral:** the famous B-29, the DC-37.

According to one rule, **single capital letter with following noun:** X-ray, B-flat, D-string. Competing and preferable open form (WNID style): X ray, B flat, D string.

**Certain proper names:** Wilkes-Barre, Winston-Salem, Stratford-on-Avon. (But Czechoslovakia, Yugoslavia, Indochina.)

It is not necessary to break up with hyphens the natural unity of such duplicating, rhyming, or alliterative words as the following: flimflam, hodgepodge, whippersnapper, knickknack, claptrap, bonbon, seesaw, zigzag. But certain words in this pattern are usually hyphened: hush-hush, goody-goody, wishy-washy, shilly-shally (noun, adjective, or verb), willy-nilly (adjective or adverb).

## Open Compound Nouns

In connected text, though perhaps not in dictionary columns, open compound nouns occur much oftener than solid and hyphened put together. They are readily and unconsciously made, and are created in such numbers that no dictionary staff could think of keeping up with them. The reading public is familiar with such names as filling stations, parking lots and parking meters, traffic laws and traffic lights, grocery stores and hardware stores, office buildings and apartment buildings, coffee cups, and so on indefinitely. These are not phrases; they are compounds. Some of the more important types of open compounds are as follows:

**Gerund and noun:** starting point, sporting goods, shipping point, melting point and freezing point, standing room, tracing cloth, swimming pool, filing case, washing machine, frying pan, carving knife. (A very numerous and increasing class of compounds, prevailingly written in open form. Hyphened forms now look archaic.)

**Abstract noun followed by another noun:** labor union, intelligence test, reference book, quality control, service record, entrance blank, insurance policy, interest table, pay envelope, tax cut, income tax.

**Mass noun followed by another noun:** cotton crop, food supply, coal mine, grain market, sugar jar, coal tar, oil refinery, steel mill, cattle pen, wood pulp, copper mining.

**Object noun and agent noun:** water cooler, shoe scraper, gas meter, copy editor. (Solid form is frequent in this pattern, especially when the second member is maker, making, master, holder, or keeper.)

**Compounds with long members:** dictionary stand, apartment building, storage cellar, investment program, index number, coral snake, pepper shaker, shoulder pad. (But solid: artilleryman, congresswoman, coralflower, coralberry, hummingbird, buttonbush. Second members of these are in the WNID list of words that readily stand as second members of solid compounds.)

**Numerous specific compounds with short members:** air line, air pump, sun lamp, sea food, sea foam, rain check, night club, night latch, price list, nest egg, roll call, nail file, rip cord. (Such compounds—they are not phrases—are familiar and readily understood.)

Though titles of office are not clearly compounds, they are usually so listed. GPO lists open forms for the following: vice president, attorney general, major general, lieutenant colonel, under secretary, commander in chief. (Alternative forms for the last two: undersecretary, commander-in-chief.)

As a general rule, appositional expressions are phrases, not compounds, and therefore take spaced form: father confessor, robber baron, robber fly, rogue elephant, major general commandant.

## COMPOUND ADJECTIVES

The most important use of the hyphen is to mark attributive adjective compounds—unit modifiers that precede their nouns: star-and-dagger indexes, three-to-em spaces, three-ton trucks, stop-loss orders, the go-ahead signal, year-in-year-out performance, month-day-year dates. Such compounds are so readily made that no dictionary can record anything like all of them.

Recognized solid compounds can also be used as unit modifiers: a commonplace remark, everyday English, hidebound conservatives, typewriter ribbons, newspaper editorials, the workaday world. And open unit modifiers are increasingly common, to the great distress of hyphen purists. More of that later.

The typical two-member compound adjective standing before its noun has primary accent on the first member, secondary accent on the second member: TEN-point type, GOLD-filled watch case, SMALL-mouthed black bass. A compound adjective that completes a verb takes a different stress pattern. Compare *bone-dry town* with *The town was bone dry.*

### Hyphened Made-to-Order Adjectives

The compounding hyphen is being increasingly used in unit modifiers made on the spot for a momentary purpose: the open-market price, off-the-record remarks, day-to-day and hour-to-hour agreements, a none-too-even-tempered dog, fly-by-night operators, the basic large-dollar-large-volume industry, the get-it-while-you-can system, run-of-the-mill specimens, a handle-with-care topic. Rudolph Flesch, whose *Art of Plain Talk* recommends this use of the hyphen as a means of lively expression, has himself used such expressions as "maiden-auntish examples," "this just-to-give-you-the-idea device," "the I-don't-really-mean-it technique." Though such coinages have their value, they can easily become a mannerism. Specimens of nonce compounds are easy to find, notably in the bright pages of *Time*.

## Other Hyphened Compound Adjectives

Unit modifiers in the following patterns—not an exhaustive list—are customarily hyphened:

**Self adjectives:** self-sustaining, self-explanatory, self-satisfied. (Note solid forms of *self* derivatives: unselfish, selfless.)

**Spelled-out numerals and fractionals:** twenty-one, ninety-ninth, a two-thirds majority. (Fractionals used as nouns are spaced: two thirds of the membership, half a dollar, a half dollar.)

**Adjective-noun phrases converted into unit modifiers:** low-grade ores, double-action revolver, a first-rate man, twelve-point type.

**Adjective, noun, and** *ed*: warm-blooded, cold-hearted, stony-hearted, thin-skinned. Or the first member may be a noun: lion-hearted, dog-eared.

**Noun and adjective:** water-soluble, fire-resistant, sky-high, mile-deep.

**Noun and passive participle:** water-borne traffic, mortgage-ridden farmers, a state-controlled press, an L-shaped part, factory-rebuilt machines, star-crossed lovers. (But usually solid: handmade, homemade.)

**Flat adverb (without** *ly*) **and passive participle:** ill-timed, above-named. (But overruled, outmoded.)

**Passive participle plus adverb or prepositional phrase:** warmed-over food, uncalled-for remarks, made-over clothing, a made-to-order suit.

**Flat adverb and present participle:** slow-burning powder, a fast-increasing rate. (But no hyphen if the adverb carries *ly*: a rapidly increasing population.)

**Coordinate nouns or adjectives:** the Dow-Jones averages, Diesel-electric locomotives, a blue-green fabric, the centimeter-gram-second system.

**Prepositional phrase or noun plus prepositional phrase:** off-color stories, three-for-a-dime apples, over-the-counter stocks, a face-to-face showdown, hand-to-mouth existence.

**Gerund and adverb:** the jumping-off place, a coming-out party.

**A and B:** tongue-and-groove joints, rough-and-tumble fighting, rough-and-ready frontiersmen.

**Verb and object noun:** stop-loss orders, stop-press news.

**Miscellaneous:** a stick-in-the-mud management, lighter-than-air machines, a head-on collision, fact-finding boards.

Whether one should write *well-behaved boys* or *well behaved boys* is a moot point. Concerning "a well known plan," the *Handbook of Style of the Princeton University Press* (1930) says, "*Well* is an adverb . . . and does not need the hyphen." But hyphenation in this pattern is more usual. In the pattern *beautifully designed cabinet* (the adverb carrying *ly*) hyphenation is archaic.

## Open Unit Modifiers

The following classes of unit modifiers require no hyphens:

**Proper names of two or more words turned into adjectives:** New Orleans newspapers, the Mardi Gras festivities, Government Printing Office styles. (If the noun carries a hyphen, this hyphen is retained: the Dow-Jones averages, a Winston-Salem newspaper.)

**Modifier enclosed in quotes:** "when issued" securities, the "favorite son" technique. If the character of the expression makes quotes unsuitable, these should not be used to save hyphenation.

**Modifier a Latin or French expression:** an ex officio member, laissez faire economics, a priori reasoning, a bona fide contract, ad hoc education, the sub rosa market.

**Certain adverb-adjective patterns:** a very much better plan, an ever dwindling supply, a very well managed affair.

**Other patterns:** fifteenth century weapons, a 10 per cent increase, a $74 million loss. (Some prefer to hyphen these.)

## Other Open Unit Modifiers

If an open compound noun is familiar (high school, insurance company, stock market, holding company, post office, public utility), it may be readily used in open form as a unit modifier: high school athletics, insurance company investments, stock market ticker symbols, post office employees, and so on. Such forms are increasingly common. Examples from the *New York Times*: consumer goods industries, world recovery plans, export license control, public utility financing transactions, cotton mill purchases. Of course one must make sure that the spaced form is clear. If not, the hyphen is available.

# DERIVATIVE WORDS

As a general rule, prefixes and suffixes in derivative words are attached to stems without hyphens: businesslike, bicarbonate, triangular, superheated, ultramicroscopic, superannuated, nonessential, nonentity. But there are exceptions for special reasons:

**Words with prefixes followed by capital letters:** un-American, non-Germanic.

**Words with duplicated prefixes:** sub-subordinate, sub-subcommittee.

**Words in which the same consonant letter occurs three times at a junction:** a bell-like tone, will-less addicts. (Awkward forms at best.)

With some exceptions, **words in which the prefix ends and the stem begins with the same vowel letter:** anti-inflation, ultra-atomic. GPO has such a rule with the important exception of the short prefixes co, de, pre, pro, re. Applying these exceptions, one writes coordinate and cooperate, deenergize, preeminent and preempt, prooptic, reenter, reenact.[4] The dieresis

---

[4] UCP style: co-operation, pre-empted, re-enter. The hyphened form *co-operation* makes possible such an atrocity as *nonco-operation*.

(as in coöperate, preëminent) is sometimes used in book printing where a vowel letter is repeated; but dieresis characters are missing from the standard typewriter keyboard and from some fonts of type.

**Expressions in which the hyphen is a useful signal of pronunciation and meaning:** co-op (cooperative enterprise), co-owner, co-author, re-creation (remaking), re-formed (formed anew).

For derivatives or phrases with *by, ex, extra, infra, non, pan, pseudo, quasi, ultra, vice,* the following GPO styles are good:

**By:** byeffect, byelection, bylaw, bypass, byproduct, byword.

**Ex:** ex post facto, ex-governor, ex-official.

**Extra:** extra-atmospheric, extraterritorial, extra-European. (Phrases with adverbial *extra*: extra mild, extra hazardous.)

**Infra:** infrared, infra-auricular.

**Non:** noncooperation, nonneutral, non-pros.

**Pan:** pan-American (but Pan American Union, official usage).

**Pseudo:** pseudo actor, pseudo accident, pseudoalkaloid, pseudo-anthropology, pseudo-Eocene. (The last three follow the GPO rule, "If second element is a technical or scientific term, make one word, using hyphen before capitalized term.")

**Quasi:** quasi authority, quasi classic.

**Ultra:** ultra-atomic, ultraconservative, ultra-Puritan, ultraviolet.

**Vice:** vice admiral, vice-admiralty, vice consul, vice-consulate, vice president, vice-presidency, viceroy, viceroyalty.

Some offices use hyphens after certain of these prefixes or words. For example, UCP specifies the following: quasi-corporation, quasi-historical; nonco-operation (but nondescript, nonessential, noncombatant); intra-urban; extra-hazardous; ultra-conservative, ultra-violet (but ultramicroscopic). Between the UCP hyphened forms and the GPO solid or spaced forms, the GPO forms are the safer choice.

## Words with Latin and Greek Elements

As a rule, words made of classical stems or combining forms such as Latin *centi* and Greek *mega* are solid: centimeter, millimeter, megacycle, thermodynamics, electromotive, kilocalorie, microampere, radioactivity, aerodynamic, photosynthesis, biochemistry, semicolon, semiannual.

## COMPOUND VERBS, ADVERBS, CONNECTIVES, AND PRONOUNS

Though long lists of solid and hyphened compound verbs could be made up from dictionary entries, open forms occur much oftener in connected text. (A sampling of 150 compound verbs and verbals taken as they came in eight well printed periodicals shows 1 hyphened, 15 solid, 134 open.) Examples of compound verbs:

**Solid:** broadcast, typewrite, streamline, blackball, whipsaw, buttonhole, pigeonhole, waterproof.

**Hyphened:** cold-chisel, cold-forge, heat-treat, spray-dry, deep-freeze, double-track, machine-drill.

**Open:** take up, take over, eke out, throw in, point out, put on, sum up, run off, pick up, pick out, lay off, lay out, lay up, give up, carry on, hold off, bring in, dispose of. (The very numerous verbs in this pattern make an important part of the English verb system.)

It is to be noted that when the adverbial part of a true compound such as *throw away* is separated from the verb, the adverb is not part of a compound. Compare these: "He *threw away* a golden opportunity" (compound verb). "He *threw* his opportunity *away*" (verb followed by object and modifier; no compound).

Gerunds such as *fishing* enter very freely into compounds:

fishing rod, trout fishing. Participles and quasi participles are also frequently used in compounds: loose-jointed, heartbroken, homespun, water-borne, silver-tongued.

Such compounds as "to deer-hunt," "to ice-skate," "to tarpon-fish" belong to informal conversation rather than to writing.

## Compound Adverbs and Connectives

Solid forms of adverbs, prepositions, and conjunctions are common: until, anyhow, somehow, sometimes, furthermore, otherwise, outside, already, altogether, wholesale (as adverb), notwithstanding, nevertheless, nonetheless, moreover, indeed, nowadays, outright, straightway, today, tonight, tomorrow. (The hyphened forms of the last three, common in the early 1900s, are now archaic.)

Open forms are also common: up to, out of, in spite of, as soon as, insofar as, inasmuch as, in order that, all right. (*All right* does not follow the analogy of *already, altogether*. Though arbitrary, custom is king.)

Hyphened adverbs, except nonce compounds, are infrequent: *well-nigh* hopeless; making long solid compounds *German-fashion*. Hyphens are unnecessary in the following: striking *head on*, stocks sold *over the counter*, wading *knee deep*.

## Compound Pronouns

There is no disagreement about pronouns ending in *self*, *ever*, or *body* (himself, itself, whoever, whichever, anybody, somebody). But certain pronouns appear in different forms: any one, anyone; some one, someone; one's self, oneself. A good rule of style is to follow GPO and WNID by using solid forms: anyone, everyone, someone, oneself. But the open form *no one* is advisable because *no* ends and *one* begins with the same vowel letter *o*.

## Suspension Hyphens

If two hyphened compounds have a second member in common, it is sometimes convenient to use the style *eight- and ten-point type, long- and short-term capital gains* (not "long and short-term gains"). This pattern, often used in good periodicals, is to be recommended more for brevity than for beauty.

For hyphens in abbreviations of hyphened compounds, see Chapter 11.

## Recommendations to Authors

1. Never hyphen or close up an expression unless it is a compound. If it is a compound, give it solid, hyphened, or open form according to circumstances. Most compound nouns are either solid or open (*footnote, fountain pen, betting odds*). Most compound adjectives preceding their nouns, except recognized solid forms such as *homespun,* are hyphened.

2. Make sure that forms are clear. Any compound that distorts the meaning or puzzles the reader is bad. If a traditional rule stands in the way of clear and excellent expression, either reword or waive the rule for the moment. (The solid form *unselfconscious* used by a ranking authority on compounding violates at least two rules. But how much better this is than *unself-conscious!*)

3. Be consistent. To this end, follow *one* stylebook or *one* good dictionary. Keep an alphabetized list of your decisions—e.g. *per cent,* p. 3; *bylaw,* p. 31; *cross section,* p. 37.

4. In close choices between hyphened and solid forms, prefer the solid forms if they have good dictionary or stylebook authority. (Such authority need not be unanimous.) In a close choice between hyphened and open forms, give the open form the benefit of the doubt. If an open form gives the same meaning that a solid form would give, the general principle is clear —do not close up.

5. If you are not an expert, give the copy editor blanket authority to make decisions, or list doubtful cases by page numbers and authorize the copy editor to decide. He is experienced and has good reference material.

6. Reduce the number of hyphened forms (a) by using solid or open forms that are listed by good authorities, (b) by rewording expressions that call for awkward hyphenation, (c) by thinking twice before you use hyphened derivatives such as *anti-inflationary, co-operation*. The solid forms *cooperation, reenter, preeminent* have good authority.

# CHAPTER 11

# DIVISION HYPHEN, APOSTROPHE, AND ABBREVIATION PERIOD

The purpose of this chapter is to outline the most important customs in line-end division of words, in the use of that troublesome little mark the apostrophe, and in abbreviated forms with or without marks of abbreviation. Because division hyphens, apostrophes, and abbreviation periods are subject to office rules for the sake of consistency and good page design, no attempt is made to give a multitude of rules for word division or any list of standard abbreviations.

## LINE-END DIVISION

"The hyphen" is a common name for the compounding hyphen (Chapter 10) and the division hyphen, which usually appear in the same form except in dictionary entries and in the standard list of proof marks. The hyphen in *self-denial* is a compounding hyphen. The hyphen at the end of a line where part of a word is carried over to the next line (e.g. the *tial* of *partial*) is a division hyphen. If *self-* stands at the end of a line and *denial* is carried over, the hyphen does double duty.

Most decisions about word division are made by printers—for which fact authors should be grateful. It is well for authors to remember that printers are crowded between the devil of bad spacing and the deep sea of undesirable division, and to be tolerant if divisions are not entirely to their taste. Theodore Low De Vinne makes the astonishing statement (*Correct Composition,* p. 141) that "the time wasted in over-

running and respacing lines to avoid divisions objected to
by proofreader and author is a serious tax upon the cost of
composition—not less in the aggregate than one fifth of the
cost of type-setting alone."

For the sake of both easy reading and good typographical
design, printers keep line-end division to the minimum that
is attainable without sacrifice of good spacing. So far as
division is necessary, their ideal may be summed up in the
following precepts. Rule 1 is basic.

1. **Divide according to pronunciation so that the part of the
   word left at the end of the line will suggest the sound and
   meaning of the whole word:** monop-oly, mono-tone, monot-
   onous, epi-taph, epit-ome, prog-ress (noun), pro-gress (verb,
   with accent on *gress*), progres-sive, change-able, tran-quil,
   per-jury, mali-cious. Despite etymology, it is often necessary
   to carry over part of a stem with the ending: reli-gious, coura-
   geous, suspi-cious, criti-cism, ungra-cious. If etymology and
   clear suggestion of sound and meaning call for the same division, so much the better: para-bolic, anti-logarithm, blacksmith, mono-graph, thermo-dynamics. Most of the following
   are applications of the basic rule

2. **Do not divide a word of one syllable:** taxed, asked, dropped,
   named, cowl, height, length, breadth.

3. **In general, divide solid compounds between the members:**
   sky-rocket, laundry-man, copper-head, hand-book.

4. **If a hyphened compound must be divided, divide on the
   hyphen, or on one of the hyphens if there are two or more:**
   vice-presidency, father-in-law (on either hyphen).

5. **Avoid misleading or ridiculous divisions:** coal-esced, unco-
   ordinated, nonco-operation, rea-dable, converti-ble.

6. **Avoid one-letter divisions; do not divide:** any, away, again,
   ago, among, enough, erode, erase.

7. **In verbals with the ending** *ing,* **usually divide before** *ing:*
   offer-ing, develop-ing, chang-ing, danc-ing, tell-ing, pull-ing,

roll-ing. But note exceptions as follows: (a) trick-ling, buck-ling, siz-zling, ruf-fling; (b) words in which a consonant letter has been doubled before the ending: admit-ting, compel-ling, prefer-ring, forbid-ding, thin-ning, stop-ping, slam-ming.

8. When two different consonant letters occur together, or when a consonant letter is doubled, usually divide between rather than after them: abun-dance, permis-sion, inflam-mable, advan-tage, exces-sive. If this rule conflicts with rule 1, the basic rule applies: swell-ing, stall-ing, tramp-ing, stick-ing, demo-cratic.

9. Preferably divide after an accented vowel rather than a light vowel: exhibi-tion, revoca-tion. But the basic rule may require division after a light vowel: episco-pal, fanati-cism.

10. Ideally, do not divide after a two-letter prefix or carry over a two-letter ending. (Subject to spacing.)

11. Do not allow more than two successive lines to end with hyphens. (Subject to spacing.)

12. Allow no hyphen at the end of a page or at the end of the next to last line of a paragraph.

Good printers do not like to divide a long numeral, a given name or surname, or a two-syllable word. But the inexorable demands of good spacing often require them to do what they don't like. Their skill in reconciling good spacing with ideal or minimum division is remarkable.

Authors can help the printer by heeding a suggestion made by John Benbow in *Manuscript & Proof*—to divide no word at the end of any line in typed copy. A division hyphen may be mistaken for a compounding hyphen and result in the hyphenation of a standard solid form such as *praiseworthy* or *hummingbird*.

The division hyphen has three minor uses: (1) to exhibit the spelling or structure of a word (s-e-p-a-r-a-t-e, ir-re-voc-able); (2) to suggest stuttering or hesitation (Y-y-es, I-I w-w-ill); (3) to represent careless or dialectal pronunciation (Come a-runnin').

## THE APOSTROPHE

The apostrophe marking the genitive, says the *New English Dictionary* (Oxford University Press), "originally marked merely the omission of *e* in writing, as in *fox's, James's,* and was equally common in the nominative plural, esp[ecially] of proper names and foreign words (as *folio's=folioes*); it was gradually disused in the latter, and extended to all possessives, even where *e* had not been previously written, as in *man's, children's, conscience' sake.* This was not yet established in 1725." The history of the apostrophe helps to explain its use as a sign of the genitive, of omissions, and sometimes of the plural.

The uses of the apostrophe are as follows:

1. **To mark, with or without** *s*, **the genitive case forms of nouns** (commonly but less accurately called the possessive case), as in *Frank's hat, the children's playthings, for conscience' sake, a day's wages.* The genitive singular is usually formed by the addition of apostrophe and *s*; but the awkward pronunciation suggested by the doubled *s* is avoided by the standard forms *for Jesus' sake, for conscience' sake,* and *Socrates' Apology.* Though the best authorities favor *Keats's poetry* and *Mr. Jones's car,* the *s* after the apostrophe has an insecure foothold in general usage. The standard custom in geographical names such as *Pikes Peak* and *Browns Ferry* is to omit the apostrophe. The possessive pronouns or adjectives *ours, yours, hers, theirs, its* take no apostrophes; but the possessive forms of indefinite pronouns are written with apostrophe: *one's responsibility, some one else's property; nobody's business.*

   **A genitive plural** is ordinarily formed by the addition of the apostrophe alone when the common plural ends in *s* (*boys'* *shoes*), otherwise by the addition of apostrophe and *s* (*women's hats, men's shoes*). But there are two exceptions. (1) The apostrophe is omitted in such names as Massachusetts Investors Trust, Teachers College at Columbia University, Merchants National Bank. (2) The apostrophe is often omitted when the word is followed by a gerund: He said something about officers being assigned to this detachment. (3) Plural genitives of measure are being written increasingly without apostrophe: ten days leave, a six months delay. (*Ten days* and *six months* in these expressions may be called open unit modifiers.) But some offices are careful to use the apostrophe: ten days' leave, a six months' delay.

2. **To mark certain standard contractions of subject and verb or verb and negative**: isn't, can't, doesn't, don't, he's, we're, it's. (The obsolescent use of the apostrophe to mark abbreviations is mentioned later under the heading Abbreviations.)

3. **To indicate special pronunciation**: unable to sleep o' nights; slim pickin's; a fishin' trip; let 'em go.

4. **To form with *s* the plurals of numerals, symbols, or letters** ("dot your i's and make your 3's unmistakable"), of words named as words ("three *very's* in one sentence"), and sometimes of abbreviations such as Y.M.C.A. A rare and clumsy use is to make plurals of classical names ending in *s* ("The Pericles' and Sophocles' of literature"). There is some latitude in the use of the apostrophe with plurals, so that an office rule is necessary—a rule, for example, specifying *the three Rs, a bid of 100.19 for 1½s*. The forms without apostrophe are gaining ground.

5. **Minor uses**: (a) The apostrophe is standard in *o'clock* and in certain proper names (*O'Neill, O'Connor*). It is not needed at the end of *Peterboro* or before the *s* in *teens*. *Teens* is the ordinary plural standing for thirteen, fourteen, and so on through nineteen. (b) The apostrophe sometimes replaces *e* in abbreviated verbs or participles: *OK'd, D.D.T.'d specimens*.

## ABBREVIATIONS

For the present purpose, abbreviations may be defined as short forms so marked as to remind the reader of the spelled-out forms. *Jas.* and *Thos.* for *James* and *Thomas* are abbreviations; *Jim* and *Tom* are not abbreviations but familiar alternative names. The usual form *percent* (or *per cent*) is better than *per cent.* (with abbreviation period) because the abbreviation mark is an unnecessary reminder of the Latin form *per centum.* Though *bus* and *plane* are shortened forms of *omnibus* and *airplane,* they are better without abbreviation marks. When *phone* is appropriate, it is better without apostrophe.

The following classes of expressions need not be marked as abbreviations:

**Cardinal and ordinal numerals:** 10, 10th, Louis XV.

**Technical symbols:** Ag (for argentum, "silver"), cos (for cosine), OE, ME, MnE (for Old English, Middle English, Modern English).

**Affixes turned into words:** economic isms; the antis and the pros.

**Stump words:** taxi, bus, plane, prom, memo. (In a college catalog one would expect *Math. 103,* the period being a reminder that the short form stands for *Mathematics.* But the student's short name *math* requires no abbreviation mark.)

**Unspaced names of government boards:** TVA, SEC, RFC.

**Names of radio stations:** WBAP, WLS. (The University of Chicago Press uses the styles WLS, N.B.C.)

There has been a marked tendency toward omission of the abbreviation period. For example, abbreviated names such as C.I.O., S.E.C., A.S.A. (American Standards Association) have been steadily moving into the dotless and unspaced forms CIO, SEC, ASA.

Except in such familiar contractions as *there's, o'clock, wasn't,* apostrophes are rarely used as marks of abbreviation. *Advt.* and *assn.* are better than *adv't, ass'n.*

When prefixes and suffixes are named, they are sometimes treated like ordinary names, sometimes marked with hyphen after (prefixes) or before (suffixes). First style: the Greek affixes *hypo* and *ism.* Second style: the Greek affixes *hypo-* and *-ism.* A rule of style for an office or a book is necessary. The style without the hyphen is good.

### The Rhetoric of Abbreviations

The following are safe rules:

1. Use abbreviated forms only when they are appropriate and in good taste. They are much less likely to be useful in connected text than in directory work, tables, footnotes, and commercial or technical matter, or in bibliographical references within parentheses. A circular of the American Standards Association gives the sensible rule, "Abbreviations should be used sparingly in text and with due regard to the context and to the training of the reader."

2. Make sure that abbreviations are readily understood. If an abbreviation is not certain to be clear, spell out.

3. Short words should be spelled out (ton, day, mile).

4. Be consistent. Use a good stylebook for this purpose (say the *Manual of Style* of the University of Chicago Press) or be guided by such a list as "Abbreviations Used in Writing and Printing" in *Webster's New Collegiate Dictionary.*

5. For the sake of clearness and consistency in abbreviations, use standard forms listed by a good stylebook or dictionary. For technical abbreviations, one needs to ascertain the practices specified by his professional society or followed by the journals in his own field. For example, writers of engineering papers may be guided by the American Standards Association circular "Abbreviations for Scientific and Engineering Terms."

6. Use ditto marks only in tabular matter.

7. When short forms are appropriate, do not apologize for them with either abbreviation periods or apostrophes: cello, **gym**, varsity, memo.

## Plurals of Abbreviations

Specimen plural abbreviations are *pp.* for *pages, vols.* for *volumes, ff.* for "and following pages" (as in *pp. 176ff.*), *cts.* for *cents*. But *ft., bu., lb., yd., bbl.* are often used for either plural or singular. In technical matter the abbreviation period is commonly omitted from such abbreviations as *bbl* (barrel or barrels) and *yd* (yard or yards).

According to office style, the apostrophe is used or omitted before *s* in plurals: Y.M.C.A.'s or Y.M.C.A.s or YMCAs; etc.'s or etc.s.

## Capitals and Hyphens in Abbreviations

The rule of the *Style Manual* of the Government Printing Office reads, "In general, an abbreviation follows the capitalization and hyphenation of the words abbreviated." An accompanying example is *ft.-lb.* for *foot-pound*. In actual practice there are so many exceptions to such a rule that one had better follow a single authority—one stylebook, one dictionary, or the customs followed by the journals of the writer's special field. Specimens from the American Standards Association circular "Abbreviations for Scientific and Engineering Terms" illustrate the fact that abbreviations do not always follow the traditional rule. The first four given here do not.

| | |
|---|---|
| foot-pound-second (system) | fps |
| kilovolt-ampere | kva |
| millilambert | mL |
| reactive kilovolt-ampere | kvar |
| ohm-centimeter | ohm-cm |
| low-pressure (as adjective) | l-p |

## Abbreviation Period with Structural Marks

If the last word of a sentence carries an abbreviation period, that period also serves as the sentence point. If the sentence calls for question mark or exclamation, the abbreviation period precedes the sentence point. (The combination is so awkward that it should be avoided.)

An abbreviation period may immediately precede comma, semicolon, or dash, or (with intervening space) a beginning parenthesis. If *i.e.* is followed by a colon, the second abbreviation point is dropped (*i.e*: and not *i.e.*:) for the sake of appearance.

# APPENDIX

# APPENDIX

## A CROSS SECTION OF PATTERNS
## AND PUNCTUATION

My purpose in this appendix is to give some quantitative information about (1) the frequency of structural marks per sentence and the relative frequencies of the various marks, (2) the relative frequencies of the basic sentence types, (3) relative frequencies of various kinds of sentence beginnings, (4) varieties of practice in the use or omission of commas after adverbial or adverbial-connective sentence openers, and (5) the grouping of sentence members in compound sentences. Because the facts have brought sharply to my attention certain differences in quality, I have ventured a few comments on the merits of certain practices.

The information I have tabulated represents too small a sampling of the practice of any single writer or periodical to warrant sweeping conclusions about the general practice of that person or journal. But the aggregate samples are numerous enough to make a cross section from which something can be learned about the grammar of current journalistic writing. Certain conclusions—supported by long observation, and by close recent observation of facts that have not been included in the tables—can be offered with certainty:

1. That heavy punctuation in the average sentence is a thing of the past, and that sentence structure has noticeably lightened in the last three decades.

2. That current journalistic writing uses a straight-line subordinating style, two marks of which are (a) a low or reasonably low average number of structural marks per sentence and (b)

a high average of unit sentences (simple and complex) and a correspondingly low average of compound sentences. (See Tables A and B.)

3. That there is considerable variety in ways of beginning sentences (Table C). The most important variation of the subject-verb-complement order is the frequent use of adverbial or adverbial-connective openers.

4. That there is much diversity in the grouping of adverbial or adverbial-connective beginnings. Many and many a comma is wasted on sentence openers that would be better without commas. (See Table D and accompanying comments.)

5. That in no-conjunction compound sentences (Table E, No. 2) the semicolon is used much oftener than comma, dash, and colon together, and that the comma in such sentences is still frowned upon by careful publishers—not merely by teachers—unless the comma is supported by a suitable pattern. (A comma splice in *Time* or *Fortune* today, or in Agnes Repplier's essays or Charles Downer Hazen's *Modern European History* some thirty years ago, is utterly different from the poor student's baby comma.)

In making up the tables I have taken the facts as they came in continuous passages or in available and usually successive numbers of the periodicals cited. A list of the material examined is given at the end of this appendix.

Some of the facts surprised me: (1) the low frequency of sentence colons—colons followed by text matter (not quotations) beginning with capitals; (2) the small proportion of unpunctuated adverbial clauses at the beginnings of sentences in certain periodicals; (3) the sharp difference of practice in the grouping of adverbial phrases used as sentence openers. For the five at the top of the list in Table D, the totals are 56 open to 17 punctuated; for the five at the foot of the list the proportions are 11 open to 38 punctuated. The first five are better models than the last five.

## TABLE A

In making up Table A (Frequencies of Structural Marks) I have omitted the following: (1) hyphens, apostrophes, en dashes (as in the expression 1917–18), commas in numerals (as in 100,999), and abbreviation periods, except where terminal duty is performed by the same period; (2) quote marks; (3) points within extracts, except points that mark the termination or interruption of the extract. For example, in the following sentence the commas after *bearer* and *Jones* and the period after *laurel* are not counted.

> It seems that Colley Cibber, when he thought he was dying, wrote to the Prime Minister, "recommending the bearer, Mr. Henry Jones, for the vacant laurel. Lord Chesterfield will tell you more of him."

Editorial brackets and ellipsis dots belong to extracts, and therefore are not counted. Brackets sometimes occur in original matter, but not in the text of the passages cited.

Footnotes and headings of all kinds, including sideheads, are excluded from the estimate.

The names are arranged according to total structural marks in 100 sentences (highest to lowest). The totals are reduced to averages per sentence (last column), figured as follows: Add 100 terminal marks to total marks used within sentences, and divide this total by 100. For example, the 2.75 average for John Fischer is the sum of 100 terminal marks and 175 marks within sentences divided by 100.

Abbreviations as follows are used in the headings: *Per* period, *Qu* question mark, *Xcl* exclamation point, *Cln* colon, *Cma* comma, *Dsh* dash, *Smc* semicolon, *Par* parentheses.

### COMMENT ON TABLE A

1. The average number of structural marks per sentence for this list runs from 2.75 (terminal marks included) to 1.73. The average is 2.15, the median 2.11. As a matter of course the

averages depend not only on skill in writing and punctuation but also in part on subject matter and personal or office styles. Some of the higher averages are partly explained by too frequent punctuation of sentence openers and by the use of the good A, B, and C style (*wheat, corn, and oats*). Some of the lower averages would be higher if commas were used before conjunctions in series (*this,*

TABLE

FREQUENCIES OF STRUCTURAL MARKS, 100

| | Terminal Marks | | | |
|---|---|---|---|---|
| | Per | Qu | Xcl | Cln |
| | . | ? | ! | : |
| John Fischer.......................... | 92 | 8 | — | — |
| *New York Times*.................... | 99 | 1 | — | — |
| *The Nation* (N. Y.)................. | 95 | 3 | 2 | — |
| Walter Lippmann................... | 100 | — | — | — |
| *Saturday Evening Post*.............. | 94 | 5 | 1 | — |
| *Collier's*........................... | 98 | 1 | — | 1 |
| *Newsweek*.......................... | 96 | 1 | — | 3 |
| W. H. Chamberlin.................. | 100 | — | — | — |
| *Life*............................... | 99 | — | — | 1 |
| Stuart Chase...................... | 97 | 3 | — | — |
| *Time*.............................. | 99 | 1 | — | — |
| Vermont Royster................... | 100 | — | — | — |
| Henley Davenport.................. | 100 | — | — | — |
| Henry Hazlitt...................... | 91 | 9 | — | — |
| John T. Flynn..................... | 97 | 2 | 1 | — |
| David Lawrence................... | 91 | 9 | — | — |
| *Christian Science Monitor*........... | 98 | 2 | — | — |
| *Wall Street Journal*................. | 95 | 5 | — | — |
| *Dallas Morning News*.............. | 96 | 3 | — | 1 |
| *Fortune*........................... | 93 | 6 | 1 | — |
| Totals...................... | 1930 | 59 | 5 | 6 |

*that, and the other* instead of *this, that and the other*) and at junctions in compound sentences where commas would be useful, especially before *but*.

2. The following marks do not appear among the 4,309 structural marks: (a) suspension dots, a specialty of fiction and advertising matter; (b) question marks or exclamations *within*

A

Sentences for Each Writer or Periodical

| Marks within Sentences | | | | | Total within sentences | Avge. all marks per sentence |
|---|---|---|---|---|---|---|
| Cma | Dsh | Smc | Par | Cln | | |
| , | — | ; | () | : | | |
| 125 | 25 | 15 | 8 | 2 | 175 | 2.75 |
| 147 | 9 | — | 12 | 1 | 169 | 2.69 |
| 128 | 15 | — | 2 | 4 | 149 | 2.49 |
| 138 | 4 | 2 | — | 1 | 145 | 2.45 |
| 126 | 8 | 8 | — | — | 142 | 2.42 |
| 124 | 5 | 3 | — | 4 | 136 | 2.36 |
| 109 | 12 | 4 | 2 | 8 | 135 | 2.35 |
| 120 | 2 | 4 | 6 | 2 | 134 | 2.34 |
| 101 | 2 | 5 | 20 | 2 | 130 | 2.3 |
| 93 | 11 | 3 | — | 4 | 111 | 2.11 |
| 73 | 5 | 5 | 12 | 16 | 111 | 2.11 |
| 81 | 7 | 8 | 6 | 2 | 104 | 2.04 |
| 90 | 7 | 1 | 4 | 1 | 103 | 2.03 |
| 80 | 4 | 1 | 10 | — | 95 | 1.95 |
| 72 | 15 | 2 | — | — | 89 | 1.89 |
| 67 | 9 | — | 2 | 2 | 80 | 1.80 |
| 70 | 7 | — | — | 1 | 78 | 1.78 |
| 58 | 14 | 1 | 2 | 1 | 76 | 1.76 |
| 69 | 3 | 1 | — | 1 | 74 | 1.74 |
| 58 | 9 | 3 | 2 | 1 | 73 | 1.73 |
| 1929 | 173 | 66 | 88 | 53 | 2309 | |

sentences; (c) brackets; (d) the ugly and nearly obsolete combinations of comma with dash, semicolon with dash, colon with dash. Though one finds suspension dots here and there in good magazine articles, there are none in the 2,000 sentences here reported. Question marks and exclamations occur only as sentence points or within quotations where by rule they are not counted. Under this same rule, ellipsis dots and brackets marking omission or insertion within quoted matter are not counted.

3. The exclamation ends only 5, the question mark 59, the sentence or paragraph colon only 6 of the 2,000 sentences. (Colons before quotations or appositives are counted among the marks *within* sentences.) The facts point to the conclusions (a) that the note of admiration is very sparingly used in factual writing today and (b) that the colon is not widely and frequently used after introductory sentences. Though a different sampling might show a larger proportion of terminal colons, it is still true that most introductory sentences end with the period, which has the merit of letting the reader go on without a "Look sharply at what's ahead."

4. Commas (1,929 of the 2,309 interior marks) do about 83 per cent of the grouping within sentences. The most frequent interior mark except the comma is the dash (173). The 88 parentheses (44 pairs) are trailed by the 66 semicolons, which might be more numerous if some of our editorial writers used a more flexible style.

5. The 53 colons used within sentences—most of them as anticipatory marks of apposition or introduction, not at junctions between members of compound sentences—are less frequent than semicolons (53 to 66). Perhaps the association of the colon with *as follows* makes it seem too stiff. It need not be stiff.

6. In order to get into quantitative form the obvious fact that good current writers save commas and give wings to their style by using far more defining than descriptive relative clauses, I counted twenty consecutive specimens in each of twenty writers or editorial departments. The count included relative clauses beginning with *who, which, that, whom,* or *whose,* or with relative suppressed; I did not count clauses with *as, such as, what, what-*

*ever,* or with any of the relative adverbs *when, whether, how.*
The results are as follows:

Defining (open) ..........................176 (88 per cent).
Descriptive (punctuated) ....................24 (12 per cent).
Relatives used in the defining clauses: *who* 39, *which* 86, *that* 31,
  *whom* 4, *whose* 1; relative suppressed, 15. (Example with
  relative suppressed: The promise *he made* was faithfully kept.)
  The 86 cases for *which* include groups with *of which, to which,*
  and so on.
Relatives used in the descriptive clauses: *who* 9, *whom* 1, *which*
  14.

7. The table on page 251 of my *Modern Punctuation* (1919),
representing 4,271 sentences by ten editorial writers or departments (1917 and 1918 material), reports 4,057 periods and 5,071
commas, commas being more frequent than periods by about 26
per cent. Table A of this appendix reports 1,930 periods and 1,929
commas. If the material of the two tables may be considered
representative, periods have gained on commas in the last three
decades—a sign that the average sentence in journalistic writing
has become somewhat lighter.

The average number of structural marks per sentence in the
tabulation of 1917–1918 material is 2.34; the average for Table A
(recent material) is 2.15.

In the tabulation of 1917–1918 material, marks used within
sentences exceed terminal marks by 34 per cent (5,729 to 4,271);
in Table A of this appendix, the 2,309 marks used within sentences exceed the 2,000 sentence marks by little more than 15 per
cent—a further sign that the average journalistic sentence is less
elaborately punctuated.

## TABLE B

Table B reports relative frequencies of unit sentences (complex with subordinate clauses, simple without subordinate clauses)
in the material used for Table A.

A complex sentence is a one-member sentence with at least one
subordinate clause that is usually but not always marked by a

subordinating word (*who, if, when*) and that carries subject and verb. Specimens, subordinate clauses in italic:

> *If the plan succeeds,* it will be widely adopted. . . . The man *who knows and knows that he knows* is a master. [Relative clause with *who* carrying a second-rank subordinate clause with *that*.] . . . Jackson's riflemen, *who had good rifles and knew how to use them,* mowed Pakenham's infantry down. [Descriptive relative clause disjoined by commas.]

## TABLE B

Frequencies of Sentence Types (100 Sentences for Each Writer or Periodical Cited)

| | Unit Types | | | Assembled Types | | | Un-classified |
|---|---|---|---|---|---|---|---|
| | Simple | Complex | Total | Compound | Complex compound | Total | |
| John Fischer...... | 40 | 37 | 77 | 11 | 11 | 22 | 1 |
| *New York Times*... | 42 | 53 | 95 | 2 | 2 | 4 | 1 |
| *The Nation* (N.Y.) | 35 | 53 | 88 | 5 | 6 | 11 | 1 |
| *Walter Lippmann*.. | 36 | 56 | 92 | 6 | 2 | 8 | — |
| *Saturday Evg. Post.* | 26 | 58 | 84 | 6 | 5 | 11 | 5 |
| *Collier's*.......... | 31 | 53 | 84 | 6 | 5 | 11 | 5 |
| *Newsweek*......... | 47 | 38 | 85 | 4 | 4 | 8 | 7 |
| W. H. Chamberlin. | 39 | 55 | 94 | 3 | 1 | 4 | 2 |
| *Life*.............. | 53 | 31 | 84 | 4 | 9 | 13 | 3 |
| Stuart Chase...... | 54 | 25 | 79 | 13 | 2 | 15 | 6 |
| *Time*............. | 47 | 20 | 67 | 15 | 5 | 20 | 13 |
| Vermont Royster.. | 44 | 47 | 91 | 1 | 5 | 6 | 3 |
| Henley Davenport. | 36 | 45 | 81 | 10 | 5 | 15 | 4 |
| Henry Hazlitt..... | 39 | 58 | 97 | 1 | — | 1 | 2 |
| John T. Flynn.... | 60 | 32 | 92 | 5 | 3 | 8 | — |
| David Lawrence... | 42 | 43 | 85 | 6 | 7 | 13 | 2 |
| *Chr. Science Monitor* | 49 | 44 | 93 | 3 | — | 3 | 4 |
| *Wall Street Journal.* | 32 | 54 | 86 | 6 | 6 | 12 | 2 |
| *DallasMorningNews* | 41 | 51 | 92 | 4 | 2 | 6 | 2 |
| *Fortune*.......... | 46 | 37 | 83 | 8 | 1 | 9 | 8 |
| Totals........ | 839 | 890 | 1729 | 119 | 81 | 200 | 71 |
| Percentages... | 41.95 | 44.5 | 86.45 | 5.95 | 4.05 | 10.0 | 3.55 |

A simple sentence has one member and no subordinate clause, subordination being managed by prepositional phrases and other groups without subject and verb. Specimens:

> Frequent use of compound sentences with *and, but,* and *so* is the mark of an immature style. . . . A committee of the State Bar of Texas will report to the state-wide highway safety conference on March 19–20. . . . Hughes Spring has no public library at all, Mr. Murphy reported. [Simple sentence with tag. In a grammar room this probably would be construed as a complex sentence.] . . . The terms of three commissioners—Robert Bayles, Edward Smith, and Henry Johnson—will expire on April 1.

A compound sentence has two or more members, each of which could stand as a sentence. The junction between members may be marked by a connective with or without punctuation, or by punctuation without connective. Specimens:

> Wheat was up and oats were down. [Connective and no point at the junction.] . . . Wheat advanced four cents, but oats were off one cent. [Comma before *but.*] . . . Stocks inched forward; bonds and preferreds lost ground. [Junction marked by semicolon without connective.]

Variants of the two-member patterns illustrated above are the complex compound type (at least one member carrying a subordinate clause) and the compound compound pattern, in which a member is divided into submembers.

The "unclassified" sentences reported in the table (3.55 per cent of the 2,000) include sentences carrying quotations, simple sentences with parentheses or tags, and amorphous sentences. "Amorphous" is not a disparaging word but a description of sentences that lack subject or verb or both.

COMMENT ON TABLE B

1. Frequent use of simple and complex sentences (the unit types), infrequent use of compound sentences with *and* or *but,* and very rare use or no use of compound sentences with *so* are marks of a mature style—and of a mature mind that thinks in unit

sentences. Use of compound sentences without conjunction is not a mark of immaturity. Ability to write compound sentences without conjunctions—with semicolons, dashes, colons, or sometimes commas at the junctions—is a mark of skill when the patterns fit the punctuation. With easy and supple wording, semicolons without conjunctions are particularly useful.

2. The unit types (simple and complex) account for 86 per cent of the total, the assembled types for only 10 per cent. The 71 "unclassified" sentences (3.55 per cent) are nearer in effect to simple or complex than to compound sentences.

3. Of the 22 assembled sentences in the John Fischer sample, exactly half are complex compound. The next highest number (*Time*, 20) is accounted for by a feature of *Time* style—free use of no-conjunction compound sentences. The lowest figures are 4 each for the *New York Times* and William Henry Chamberlin, 3 for the *Christian Science Monitor,* and 1 for Henry Hazlitt.

4. Sentences with connective *for* have been tabulated as compound despite the fact that some grammarians consider *for* a subordinating conjunction in the same class with *as* and *because.* So far as punctuation is concerned, *for* behaves like *and, but, or,* and *nor,* except that *for* is regularly preceded by some punctuation mark.

5. A separate tabulation of 100 newslead sentences in the *Wall Street Journal* (issues of September 2, 5, and 6, 1947) shows 66 simple, 32 complex, only 2 compound. Only 6 of the 100 carry tags. Though a different sampling might show a somewhat larger proportion of compound sentences, it is true in general that most newslead sentences are either simple or complex, the compound type being usually too loose for the purpose. A newspaper man who doesn't know how to subordinate won't last long.

Table E gives further information about compound sentences.

## TABLE C

Table C, representing the samples reported for 14 of the 20 writers or periodicals listed in Tables A and B, tabulates sentence beginnings under five heads:

1. Subject beginnings in various forms. The most frequent type.

2. Adverbial or adverbial-connective beginnings, second in frequency and very important for clear connection. These include sentence adverbs (*certainly, perhaps*); adverbial connectives (*however, moreover*); subordinate clauses with *if, when, though,* and other subordinating words; and a great variety of phrases carrying ideas of time, place, purpose, and so on.

3. The class "conjunctions" is limited, perhaps arbitrarily, to *and, but, for, or, nor, so,* and *yet.* The favorite is usually *but.*

4. Tabulated under "other" are anticipatory *it* and *there* (usually giving notice that the subject follows the verb), 59 cases; loosely attached participial groups, 19; complements of the verb, 8; verbs, 32; responsives, 3. The total of these is 121.

TABLE C

KINDS OF SENTENCE BEGINNINGS (100 SENTENCES FOR EACH
WRITER OR PERIODICAL)

| | Subject | Adv. or Adv. con. | Conj. | Other | Unclassified |
|---|---|---|---|---|---|
| W. H. Chamberlin.... | 59 | 18 | 10 | 13 | — |
| *Dallas Morning News*.. | 69 | 15 | 8 | 8 | — |
| *Fortune*.............. | 51 | 28 | 7 | 10 | 4 |
| John Fischer.......... | 44 | 41 | 7 | 7 | 1 |
| Henry Hazlitt........ | 45 | 29 | 11 | 15 | — |
| Walter Lippmann..... | 49 | 33 | 14 | 4 | — |
| *Life*................. | 58 | 31 | 9 | 1 | 1 |
| David Lawrence...... | 61 | 15 | 10 | 13 | 1 |
| *Newsweek*........... | 42 | 36 | 10 | 9 | 3 |
| *New York Times*...... | 56 | 28 | 10 | 6 | — |
| *The Nation* (N. Y.)... | 53 | 24 | 9 | 12 | 2 |
| *Saturday Evening Post*. | 48 | 36 | 6 | 9 | 1 |
| *Time*................ | 57 | 31 | 3 | 6 | 3 |
| *Wall Street Journal*.... | 51 | 25 | 16 | 8 | — |
| Totals........... | 743 | 390 | 130 | 121 | 16 |
| Approximate percentages....... | 53 | 28 | 9 | 9 | 1 |

5. The "unclassified" beginnings, 16 in all, are in amorphous sentences and in sentences beginning with quotations or with reversed appositives. (Example of a reversed appositive: *An expert statistician,* he detected the fallacy at once.) Such inverted appositives usually have adverbial force, and might well have been included among the adverbial beginnings.

Abbreviations used in the headings of Table C are as follows: *Adv.* for adverbial expressions, whether single words or groups; *Adv. con.* for adverbial-connective words or groups; *Conj.* for conjunctions.

### COMMENT ON TABLE C

1. The percentages of subject beginnings run from 69 to 42, with an average of 53.

2. Percentages of adverbial or adverbial-connective beginnings run from 41 to 15, with an average of 28. In every case they are more numerous than any other kind of beginning except subject, doubtless because they are so useful for clear connection and suspense, directing attention to following words. Writers who do not know how to use such beginnings don't know their business.

3. The conjunctions *but, and,* and others in smaller numbers account for 9 per cent of the beginnings. In close choices between period and semicolon before a conjunction, the odds are greatly in favor of a sentence break.

4. The low proportion of verb beginnings (32 in 2,000 sentences) is explained by the fact that relatively few of the sentences are in interrogative form and that few use imperative verbs.

5. The aggregate of "other" beginnings nearly equals the total of conjunction beginnings. Though much less frequent than adverbial openers, they are useful variants. For example, anticipatory *it* or *there* can emphasize the grammatical subject by keeping the reader waiting for it.

## TABLE D

Table D, Grouping of Adverbial or Adverbial-Connective Expressions at Beginnings of Sentences, reports the grouping of 20 cases of all kinds for each of 20 writers or periodicals in the order highest to lowest number of unpunctuated sentence openers. The number of unpunctuated openers runs from 17 to zero.

The clauses include groups with subject and verb, subordinated by such words as *if, when, though, while,* and prepositional phrases carrying subordinate clauses (e.g. *in the form it finally took*).

Phrases include verbless expressions such as *in New York, six months earlier, even before the war, in any event, in short, for that reason, for this purpose.* These occur in various lengths and

TABLE D

GROUPING OF ADVERBIAL OR ADVERBIAL-CONNECTIVE EXPRESSIONS
AT BEGINNINGS OF SENTENCES (20 CASES FOR EACH
WRITER OR PERIODICAL)

| | Clauses | | Phrases | | Single words | | Totals, all kinds | |
|---|---|---|---|---|---|---|---|---|
| | Open | Pointed | Open | Pointed | Open | Pointed | Open | Pointed |
| *Fortune*, editorials..... | 2 | — | 15 | 3 | — | — | 17 | 3 |
| Frederick Lewis Allen.. | 0 | 1 | 12 | 5 | 0 | 2 | 12 | 8 |
| Stuart Chase.......... | 2 | 4 | 10 | 4 | — | — | 12 | 8 |
| *Chr.Sci.Mon.*,editorials | 2 | 4 | 10 | 4 | — | — | 12 | 8 |
| W. H. Chamberlin | ? | 4 | 0 | 1 | 1 | 0 | 12 | 8 |
| Walter Lippmann..... | 2 | 5 | 7 | 5 | 1 | — | 10 | 10 |
| Vermont Royster...... | 2 | 4 | 6 | 6 | — | 2 | 8 | 12 |
| *Life*, editorials........ | 0 | 6 | 6 | 4 | 1 | 3 | 7 | 13 |
| Henry Hazlitt......... | 0 | 7 | 6 | 6 | 1 | — | 7 | 13 |
| John Fischer.......... | 0 | 4 | 7 | 4 | — | 5 | 7 | 13 |
| *Barron's*,How'sBusiness? | 0 | 2 | 5 | 5 | 2 | 6 | 7 | 13 |
| *Time*, National Affairs. | 0 | 4 | 7 | 9 | — | — | 7 | 13 |
| *U.S. News*........... | 1 | 0 | 5 | 12 | — | 2 | 6 | 14 |
| *Sat. Evg. Post*, editorials | 0 | 5 | 6 | 8 | — | 1 | 6 | 14 |
| Frank L. Kluckhohn... | 0 | 4 | 5 | 9 | — | 2 | 5 | 15 |
| *WallStreetJournal*,news | 1 | 6 | 3 | 7 | — | 3 | 4 | 16 |
| Ernest K. Lindley..... | 2 | 5 | 2 | 7 | — | 4 | 4 | 16 |
| *Wall St. Jour.*, editorials | — | 7 | 4 | 3 | — | 6 | 4 | 16 |
| Henley Davenport..... | — | 5 | 2 | 10 | — | 3 | 2 | 18 |
| *The Nation* (N.Y.), editorials.......... | — | 5 | — | 11 | — | 4 | — | 20 |
| Totals............ | 16 | 82 | 127 | 123 | 6 | 46 | 149 | 251 |

carry a great variety of ideas—time, place, purpose, condition, and so on.

The single words include simple adverbs and connective adverbs—*nowadays, today, evidently, sometimes, accordingly, unfortunately, apparently, certainly,* and various others.

The following were not included: (a) interrogative adverbs such as *why* and *when*; (b) adverbial or adverbial-connective expressions preceding parenthetical groups. Interrogative adverbs are normally open, and a parenthetical group takes its own punctuation.

### COMMENT ON TABLE D

1. Figures for openers in clause form are as follows:

|  | Open | Punctuated with comma |
|---|---|---|
| For the whole group............ | 16 | 82 |
| For the first five................ | 8 | 13 |
| For the last five................ | 3 | 28 |

2. For openers in phrase form (2 or more words, no subject and verb) the figures are as follows:

|  | Open | Punctuated with comma |
|---|---|---|
| For the whole group............ | 127 | 123 |
| For the first five............... | 56 | 17 |
| For the last five................ | 11 | 38 |

3. For one-word openers (*thus, next, similarly, certainly, perhaps,* and so on) the figures are:

|  | Open | Punctuated with comma |
|---|---|---|
| For the whole group............ | 6 | 46 |
| For the first five................ | 1 | 5 |
| For the last five................ | 0 | 20 |

4. The totals of all kinds show that there is great diversity of practice. Some writers and copy editors appear to act on the theory that all adverbial clauses and most adverbial phrases at

the beginning must be set off. (In punctuation as in other matters, either "some" or "many" is a safer word than "all.") Writers who use good judgment punctuate according to thought and desired degrees of distinctness, not on the principle "Here's the pattern; apply the rule." For example, the writers of *Fortune* editorials and the "Atlantic Report on the World Today" in the *Atlantic Monthly* know well when an adverbial opener should be open and when it should be made distinct by punctuation.

## TABLE E

Table E (Punctuation at Junctions in Two-Member Compound Sentences) supplements Table B by reporting marks used before connectives and marks at junctions where there are no connectives. Considering that the unit types outnumber compound sentences about 9 to 1, the material searched for the 400 cases amounts to something like 4,000 sentences.

The marks reported are those occurring at the junctions in compound sentences with simple members, in complex compound sentences, and at the main junctions in compound compound sentences. (The compound compound pattern is relatively infrequent.)

### COMMENT ON TABLE E

1. In the 298 sentences with connectives at the junctions, the connectives are *and* (167 cases), *but* (95), *for* (19), *or* (8), *but* after *not only* (2), *nor* (2), *or* after *either* (1), *so* (1), *yet* (1), *otherwise* (1), *then* (1). (*So, yet, otherwise,* and *then* are much more likely to occur after sentence breaks than within compound sentences).

2. In 40 of the 167 cases with *and*, there is no mark before the connective; in only 6 of the 95 with *but* is punctuation lacking. Being more clearly disjunctive than *and, but* is much more likely to need a punctuation mark. Before either *but* or *and*, it is more usual to punctuate than to omit punctuation (216 to 46); and some of the sentences with no mark before *and* or *but* would have been easier to read if marks had been used. (It is probable that

## TABLE E

PUNCTUATION AT JUNCTIONS IN TWO-MEMBER COMPOUND SENTENCES

| Connective | No mark | Comma | Semi-colon | Dash | Colon | Total cases |
|---|---|---|---|---|---|---|
| **1. Marks Used Before Connectives** | | | | | | |
| and | 40 | 93 | 22 | 12 | — | 167 |
| but | 6 | 66 | 22 | 1 | — | 95 |
| but after *not only* | 2 | — | — | — | — | 2 |
| or | 2 | 3 | 2 | 1 | — | 8 |
| or after *either* | 1 | — | — | — | — | 1 |
| for | — | 16 | 2 | 1 | — | 19 |
| nor | — | 2 | — | — | — | 2 |
| so | — | 1 | — | — | — | 1 |
| yet | — | 1 | — | — | — | 1 |
| otherwise | — | — | 1 | — | — | 1 |
| then | — | — | 1 | — | — | 1 |
| Totals | 51 | 182 | 50 | 15 | 0 | 298 |

**2. No Connectives at Junctions**

Junctions marked by comma...................... 9
"       "       " semicolon..................... 75
"       "       " colon...................... 13
"       "       " dash...................... 5
Total............................. 102

Total cases with or without connectives.................... 400

writers who use the A, B and C style carry this style over to two-member compound sentences on the mistaken idea that sentence members ought to be treated like nouns in series.)

3. In no-conjunction compound sentences, the marks used are semicolon (75), colon (13), comma (9), dash (5). The semicolons outnumber the aggregate of the others 75 to 27. The colon does not appear at all in the list of sentences with conjunctions; the marks used in these are comma, semicolon, and dash.

4. The sentences using conjunctions outnumber the no-conjunction sentences 298 to 102. Some of our journalists—including

good men who know what's going on in the world—could improve their writing by making more use of the swift and easy patterns that call for no *and* or *but*. To mark the junctions in such sentences one has the colon (useful if the first member is clearly an introduction to the second), the dash and the comma (both to be used with care), and the indispensable semicolon.

## MATERIAL REPORTED IN THE TABLES

Except as noted, illustrative material was originally published in 1947 and the texts used are originals.

Tables A and B are based on 100-sentence samples from each of the following twenty writers and periodicals. Fourteen of the same samples are the basis of Table C.

William Henry Chamberlin, in the *Wall Street Journal*. Articles August 28 and September 5, and the first 33 sentences of book review September 22.

Stuart Chase, in *Harper's Magazine*, February 1940. Article "Capital Not Wanted," to sixth sentence break in column 1, page 228.

*Christian Science Monitor*, editorials July 1, and July 3 to second sentence break in third paragraph of "The War Debt Tide Turns."

*Collier's*, editorials, September 6, 13, and 20.

*Dallas Morning News*, editorials, September 17, and first four sentences September 18.

Henley Davenport in *Barron's*, August 18 and 25, and first six sentences September 1.

John Fischer in *Harper's Magazine* for May, article "The Lost Liberals" to last period on page 388.

John T. Flynn in *Harper's Magazine*, February 1940, article "Can Hitler Beat American Business?" to seventh period in first column on page 324.

*Fortune* editorial, July, second paragraph to period in third line above second paragraph break in third column of page 3.

Henry Hazlitt, Business Tides articles in *Newsweek*, July 28, August 11 (first sentence only), August 18, September 8.

David Lawrence, editorials in *United States News*, August 29, September 5 through first paragraph in column 3.

*Life* editorials, July 28, August 4 to period in eighth line after second paragraph break in column 2.

Walter Lippmann, *U. S. Foreign Policy*, 1943, page 3 to first period after first paragraph break on page 17.

*The Nation* (New York), editorials, July 26 (first seven sentences), August 23.

*New York Times*, editorials, September 11 to first sentence break in "A Dwindling Army."

*Newsweek*, National Affairs, August 25, to first period in "Gold Baloney," page 17.

Vermont Royster in *Wall Street Journal*, September 3 and 8, and first seven sentences September 16.

*Saturday Evening Post*, editorials, September 6, 13; first four sentences September 20.

*Time*, National Affairs, September 25, to period in ninth line after second paragraph break on page 17, column 1.

*Wall Street Journal*, editorials, August 29, September 2 through first paragraph of "Looking into Cooperatives."

Table D is based on notes of twenty adverbial openers (aggregate of the three kinds) in each of the following:

Frederick Lewis Allen, article "One Day in History," *Harper's Magazine*, November 1937. Text in Stewart Morgan's *Opinions and Attitudes in the Twentieth Century*.

*Barron's*, How's Business? September 8.

William Henry Chamberlin in *Wall Street Journal*, August 28, September 2, 5, 9.

Stuart Chase, article "This Age of Plenty," *Harper's Magazine*, March 1934. Text in Stewart Morgan's *Opinions and Attitudes in the Twentieth Century*.

*Christian Science Monitor*, editorials, June 30, July 1, 3.

Henley Davenport in *Barron's*, August 18, 25, September 1.

John Fischer, article "The Lost Liberals," *Harper's Magazine* for May.

*Fortune*, editorial, July.

Henry Hazlitt, Business Tides, *Newsweek*, March 31, April 28, July 28.

Frank L. Kluckhohn, article "Moscow's Beachhead," *Saturday Evening Post*, September 13.

*Life*, editorials, July 21, 28, August 18.

Ernest K. Lindley, Washington Tides, *Newsweek*, March 31, April 28, May 6, July 14.

Walter Lippmann, passage from *The Good Society*, 1937. Text in Stewart Morgan's *Opinions and Attitudes in the Twentieth Century*.

*The Nation* (New York), editorials, August 9, 16.

Vermont Royster in *Wall Street Journal*, September 3, 8.

*Saturday Evening Post*, editorials, September 6, 13.

*Time*, National Affairs, August 18.

*United States News*, first and second unsigned articles, August 29.

*Wall Street Journal*, editorials, September 3, 8; major news stories on first page, September 6.

The writers and periodicals represented by Table E and the number of cases for each are as follows:

Frederick Lewis Allen in *Harper's Magazine*, 24; Cleveland Amory in *Harper's Magazine*, 27; Atlantic Report on the World Today in *Atlantic Monthly*, 23; William Henry Chamberlin in *Wall Street Journal*, 12; Stuart Chase in *Harper's Magazine*, 14; editorials in *Christian Science Monitor*, 21; editorials in *Collier's*, 10; Henry Steele Commager in *Harper's Magazine*, 23; Henley Davenport in *Barron's*, 11; John Fischer in *Harper's Magazine*, 21; John T. Flynn in *Harper's Magazine*, 8; editorial in *Fortune*, 27; *Style Manual* of the Government Printing Office, 25; David Lawrence, editorial in *United States News*, 12; editorials in *Life*, 10; Walter Lippmann in *U. S. Foreign Policy*, 8; editorials in *The Nation* (New York), 10; *Newsweek*, National Affairs, 23, and Henry Hazlitt, Business Tides, 1; editorials in *New York Times*, 17; Fletcher Pratt in *Harper's Magazine*, 16; editorials in *Saturday Evening Post*, 11; *Time*, National Affairs, 27; *Manual of Style* of the University of Chicago Press, 7; editorials in *Wall Street Journal*, 12.

# INDEX OF AUTHORITIES AND PERIODICALS CITED

# SUBJECT INDEX